the social
EXECUTIVE

how to master social media
and why it's good for business

DIONNE KASIAN-LEW

WILEY

First published in 2014 by John Wiley & Sons Australia, Ltd
42 McDougall St, Milton Qld 4064

Office also in Melbourne

Typeset in 12/14.5 pt Bembo Std

© Dionne Kasian-Lew 2014

The moral rights of the author have been asserted

National Library of Australia Cataloguing-in-Publication data:

Author:	Kasian-Lew, Dionne, author.
Title:	The Social Executive: How to Master Social Media and Why it's Good for Business / Dionne Kasian-Lew.
ISBN:	9780730312895 (pbk.)
	9780730312901 (ebook)
Notes:	Includes index.
Subjects:	Communication in management.
	Businesspeople — social networks.
	Business enterprises — computer networks.
	Online social networks.
Dewey Number:	658.45

Cover design and illustration: Wiley

Author photo: © Eric Algra

ManageFlitter screenshots © ManageFlitter Pty Ltd.

Scoop.it screenshots © Scoop.it - http://scoop.it

SlideShare, the SlideShare logo, LinkedIn, and the IN logo are trademarks or registered trademarks of LinkedIn and its affiliates. All rights reserved.

Printed in Singapore by C.O.S. Printers Pte Ltd

10 9 8 7 6 5 4 3 2 1

Disclaimer

The material in this publication is of the nature of general comment only, and neither purports nor intends to be advice. Readers should not act on the basis of any matter in this publication without considering (and if appropriate, taking) professional advice with due regard to their own particular circumstances. The author and publisher expressly disclaim all and any liability to any person, whether a purchaser of this publication or not, in respect of anything and of the consequences of anything done or omitted to be done by any such person in reliance, whether whole or partial, upon the whole or any part of the contents of this publication.

This book is dedicated to those I love most—
Paul, Michael and James.

'The best CEOs lead by example and this applies to social media as well. I've always found it ironic, if not hypocritical, for Leaders to talk about being human, transparent and engaged, but who have failed to embrace social media. CEOs who don't embrace social media as a leadership tool are failing themselves and those they lead.'

Mike Myatt, America's Top CEO Coach, leadership adviser to *Fortune* 500 CEOs, *Forbes* columnist and author *Hacking Leadership* (personal email)

'first commitment as CEO ... I won't wait 4 years between tweets!'

Satya Nadella, CEO Microsoft (tweet)

'CEOs who shun social media risk losing touch with some of their most lucrative customers, prospects and influencers.'

Josh James, founder and CEO, DOMO

'The impact of the Internet on business will continue to increase massively. CEOs will need to understand their customers and the environment that their customers live and work in—which will be increasingly "social". Your brand as a CEO and as a company through social media will be key to attracting the right talent. The principal lesson that I've learned is to always be learning and never believe that you know enough.'

Reid Hoffman, chairman, LinkedIn

'IBM Study: If You Don't Have a Social CEO, You're Going to be Less Competitive.'

Mark Fidelman, *Forbes* columnist

'C-level executives vary considerably in their perceptions about the value of social business. On average (across most industries), CEOs, presidents, managing directors, board members, and CMOs are most likely to perceive social business as important. Indeed, CEOs are nearly twice as likely as CIOs and CFOs to view social tools as important to their business today.'

Deloitte, *Wall Street Journal*

*By the time you finish reading this book,
the data will have changed...*

Contents

About the author

Dionne Kasian-Lew is CEO of The Social Executive, a thought leader, author and professional speaker on connected leadership and communication.

A graduate of the Australian Institute of Company Directors, she is an adviser and coach to board and C-suite executives on leadership and digital and social media strategy.

Dionne is a regular contributor to web publications *Leading Company*, *Smart Company*, *Women's Agenda* and to Salesforce. She also writes for *Company Director*, Uncluttered White Spaces and Firebrand Talent, and on dionnekasianlew.com and beyourwholeself.com.

She is the author of *A manifesto—why social media is vital for leaders* and the ebook *Relevance—how to thrive in the social era*.

Follow Dionne on Twitter @dionnelew.

Acknowledgements

This is a chance to thank the people who have influenced my thinking and supported my online journey:

- Dan Ilic — for pushing me over the cliff to begin with
- Trevor Young — for unfailing support and brilliant coaching
- Kare Anderson — for serendipitous and synergising connection.

I also want to thank those who have no idea of their influence on my thinking:

- John Brockman (Edge)
- Maria Popova (Brainpicker)
- Chris Anderson (Ted)
- … and the incredible, interconnected communities I engage with every day online.

My thanks to the true pioneers who pushed across this frontier without waiting to be legitimated — and so laid the foundations on which we have all been able to flourish.

On a more personal note, thanks to Katie Elliott, Wiley's delightful publicist, a cool and connected communicator who first found me on Twitter and sparked this journey. Katie pretty much embodies the principles I talk about in this book—how social connections lead to meaningful and mutually beneficial business outcomes.

To Sarah Crisp, for listening to me and taking a chance on my work, and Lucy Raymond for stepping in where Sarah left off and supporting me throughout the process.

To the Wiley team—Dani Karvess, Fleur Hamilton, Pete Walmsley, Keira de Hoog and everyone who helped to bring this book to life—my gratitude.

Thank you, Jem Bates, for editing *The Social Executive* and guiding me through the publication process.

Walter Adamson, Ben Gilchriest and Trevor Young gave their precious time and attention to read, review and make suggestions on the manuscript. Your insights were invaluable and much appreciated.

And to all my clients—for leading from the edge and by example, and teaching me along the way.

Last, I want to thank my sisters Michelle and Kim, whose ongoing love and support throughout my life have helped me thrive. Alphonse, Mark, Lily, Cy, Xabi and Mum—thank you. You mean the world to me.

Introduction

Around the world, time and again research into social media and leadership reveals the same insights:

1 Executives know that social media is vital.

2 They know they need to do something about it.

3 They want to know why and how.

This book delivers on those needs. Starting with powerful evidence from the best global consultancies on the magnitude of the multi-trillion-dollar connected economy, it separates the myths from the facts and provides a practical guide for professionals to move forward and capitalise on its opportunities.

Reading *The Social Executive* will arm you for social engagement and the digital economy by showing you how to:

- *Bust the myths.* Separate the facts from the fiction. You will learn that social media is not a fad but is growing rapidly and becoming deeply entrenched in business. For example, the LinkedIn business network is 12 years old and used by 250 million professionals around the world.

- *Speak C-suite social.* Build evidence-driven arguments based on incisive analysis for socialising business. You will be able to articulate its value by referring to real case studies that show its impact in your industry.

- *Walk your social talk.* Understand the key social media platforms, what they are used for and why. You'll be able to distinguish Twitter from Facebook and SlideShare from LinkedIn without resorting to jargon, and to speak sensibly about emerging issues like privacy and security and how they can be effectively managed through good governance.

- *Take a seat at the social table.* Launch a personal professional platform. Learn how to use the five networks that deliver tangible results for executives. Avoid pitfalls and use powerful tips from master practitioners to move you swiftly from newbie to proficiency.

While technology has in some ways turned business on its head, at heart it's based on the age-old business principles of mutually beneficial relationships and great communication.

Time and again you'll hear me preface a comment by saying 'as in real life' and showing you how these innovations compare to established professional practices. There's no mystique to social media. But there is magic. As in real life, so too in the digital world.

This book directly addresses two core questions that professionals have about social media: Why is social media important, and how do I use it?

In Part I you'll learn why, given the magnitude and growth of the digital economy, becoming a social executive is an essential professional investment. You'll also learn how to remove blocks that may have stopped you from capitalising on this. Each chapter identifies a part of the puzzle and points readers towards particular solutions.

In Part II I'll show you how to snap up valuable digital assets and grow online influence by creating a curated and automated professional platform.

The Social Executive is not:

- a catalogue of social media networks
- a technical operating manual.

If it's here, then it's information that helps professionals or raises questions that count.

I've selected proven tools for growing online influence that fit with a busy schedule. At the end of the practical how-to chapters (9–13) are Bootcamp tools to help take you to the next level, once your Professional Platform is established. Going through every setting and what lies behind it would be tedious, time-consuming and unnecessary. I show you how to get up and running.

By the end of the book you will have a Professional Platform and a replicable strategy that will guarantee you a constant global social media presence, increased online visibility and influence, and a range of valuable online colleagues with whom to share ideas and information.

A note on terminology

Stuffing sentences with caveats to try to cover every base causes lag. Here's a (sadly not unusual) example:

> Board directors, senior executives and professionals need to understand that social media networks and other social and digital technologies like apps are deeply impacting the way we do business and that, going forward, companies will need to socialise processes and systems in order to develop an integrated social business model.

Yawn! Who can bear it? In this book I have taken the liberty of using terms loosely and exchanging them freely. Here are some longwinded descriptions of what I mean when I use these key terms—you'll have no problem with context:

- *Social media*. When using this term I am talking about social media networks like Twitter and LinkedIn, but more broadly about the connections that social technologies generate and that impact business, economies and societies. Social media is a tool *and* a mindset. *Going social* means sending a tweet but also becoming a social professional or business, end to end.

- *Digital.* This refers to that whole layer of stuff that's not analogue, including online software, information, content, websites and apps, but also connected networks such as social media, forums and blogs. I am not talking about hardware or technology infrastructure, which is IT — critically important, but not for this book. Executives need to stop confusing IT with social media, though. Social media does not sit on your web, although it can be embedded in it. Platforms belong to third parties, and you can access them under their terms and conditions. Digital is not about IT, nor is it the realm of the traditional chief information officer (CIO), although there are lots of discussions about the changing nature of that role.

- *Technology.* Here I am talking about all of the above, including the internet and devices that we use to connect with it.

- *Business.* This relates to for-profit and not-for-profit, listed and unlisted companies, startups and small to medium-sized enterprises (SMEs), but also to organisations, associations, government departments, statutory authorities and charities. And I use them interchangeably. When I talk about the bottom line, simply substitute your organisation's vision. The customer is the reason you exist, whether they buy your bread or read your report or need to engage with you to do their tax. You are a customer too.

- *Executive.* This may be anyone who makes or wants to make decisions at work. Leaders are included, although executives are not to be confused with leaders because leadership is not about position. Really I am talking about people who work, because here the personal and professional merge. A social executive is one who connects online, but executives are also social offline. As the world becomes increasingly connected the distinction will become less relevant. But that's not quite yet.

- *C-suites.* These may include the chief executive officer (CEO), chief customer officer (CCO), chief marketing officer (CMO), chief financial officer (CFO), chief operating officer (COO), chief information officer (CIO) and chief legal officer (CLO).

Let's fix this problem

Right now there's a problem we can fix. More than two billion people use social media—but not the leaders who need to. They don't have the right information or don't understand that just because they're doing well without it, that situation won't last. That's because the billions of new consumers coming onto the market will have never lived in a world without it.

Let's look at this a bit more closely.

The number of people using social media increased by 18 per cent in 2013, with predictions it will soon reach 2.55 billion. While global social media platforms profoundly change the way we connect, communicate and do business, decision-makers aren't there. They know they should be but they are not—yet.

In 2012 only 16 per cent of *Fortune* 500 CEOs used social media. Mostly they signed up but did not actively use it, which is like standing in the corner at a business lunch. The reluctance? Wild confusion around what social media is and does.

Who can blame them? There's endless misinformation about social media: it's a fad or only for kids, or there's no way to measure return on investment. None of this is true. But there are barriers to getting the real story to the executive table.

Professionals hear about social media when something goes wrong and makes the traditional news channels. Perhaps there's an online troll, which reinforces fear that going social is dangerous; or you hear about a cute cat video with a billion hits, entrenching the idea of its irrelevance to the bottom line.

It's difficult to distinguish fact from fiction and genuine experts from interlopers moving in to capitalise on the chaos. Also, many leaders look around and think they and their peers are doing fine without using social media. But they're not looking in the right direction — it's about what is coming over the hill.

Millennials with votes to cast and money to spend have never lived in a world without social media. They expect you to be social not because you're cutting edge or socially savvy but by default, much as shops once required inventory and a front door.

We talk about digital natives, those who have grown up with technology, as if they come from a different world. But this is nothing compared with the generations now coming online who will be symbiotic with it.

It's urgent that executives see beyond the myths and capitalise on the personal and professional opportunities that connection provides. Social media is part of a bigger picture of socialising business, which in turn is a part of a much bigger picture of interconnectivity across economies, politics, business, knowledge, health ... and pretty much every other aspect of life.

The impact of social media on political outcomes or sharemarkets is so dramatic that countries are legislating to make it a board and C-suite responsibility.

For example, in the US in 2012 billions of dollars changed hands after a hoax tweet about a bomb at the White House. A false accusation that a British politician was a pedophile spread far and fast, the head of the British Broadcasting Corporation (BBC) was forced to resign and tens of thousands of Twitter users were under threat of being sued. In Australia, AUS$350 million was wiped off the share price of Whitehaven Coal after an activist issued a hoax tweet.

Yet many directors and executives don't understand that the ball for monitoring and managing these risks is in their court.

Managing risk is one half of the equation. There's solid evidence that organisations that see digital as a way of being, rather than a handball-to-marketing, outperform their peers by 26 per cent in every industry. These firms are distinguished from competitors by their digitally driven board and executives prepared to propel change through every layer of the business.

In the past a succession plan would have identified the need for digital capability in emerging leaders. Today the accelerated speed of change and the rapid adoption of new technologies mean delay is dangerous. Many executives know something major is happening but have not yet translated this into action. The fear of technology is unwarranted. Professionals constantly adapt, and digital and social literacies are skills that can be learned.

Leaders must act to create business models with a competitive advantage by understanding that social media is not about a 'like' on Facebook or a 140-character 'tweet', but about the future of how we do business.

By engaging in social media you come to understand its power. It will change your mindset. But best of all, if you're like many I know who've made a transition from reluctant observer to engaged participant, you'll love it.

And one problem will be fixed.

Part I

WHY IS SOCIAL MEDIA IMPORTANT?

Social media has been called a fad, a distraction for teenagers or at best a pleasant but unprofitable waste of time. The truth is it has introduced a dramatic shift in the way we engage that is turning business on its head. For those who know how to use it properly, social media offers an unparalleled business opportunity and is critical for success in an interconnected world.

Read the following chapters to learn:

- how big the digital economy already is, how it will continue to grow and how you can leverage that for business success
- six damaging myths that have deterred executives from adopting social media and facts that will change your mind about it
- how to evolve beyond traditional management thinking to a social growth mindset
- how much social absenteeism costs professionals
- legal reasons why every executive must understand social media, even if they don't like it and don't wish to
- how to leverage social media for professional development and career growth.

CHAPTER I

Gargantuan and growing: the digital economy

The current focus on social media has many leaders wondering about its impact on their careers and businesses. They are asking:

- Is this a structural change or just a fad?
- Does it impact the whole economy or just particular industries?
- Does it apply across a business or just to sales?
- Is it the right time to invest in social platforms?
- What's it worth?
- How, if at all, does social media contribute to productivity and the bottom line?

Let me paint the picture.

How connected are we?

The number of people online has doubled since 2007 to 2.55 billion, and 91 per cent of them use social or mobile networks. That's an awe-inspiring number, but it's just the start of a steep trajectory.

More than half of the world has yet to come on board, but they are doing so now, to the tune of eight new users a second (that means around 40 new people came online while you were reading that sentence). In developing countries in particular, new users are skipping the path we took through analogue and hardwired technologies and going straight to digital, mobile, social.

Just as you've never lived in a world without cars and think of the horse-and-cart as historically quaint, so billions have never lived without hyper-connection. Would you tether a horse to a cart? Take it to a meeting across town? Could you even do so if you wanted to? I imagine not. So why do we expect others will want to connect with us on antiquated systems?

There are more devices connected to the web than there are people on Earth, using more kinds of devices than ever before. We are using smartphones, tablets, laptops, wearable technologies—and that's before we get started on the emerging 'Internet of Things' that connects everything to everything else and everyone to it. According to industry analyst firm IDC, the installed base for the Internet of Things will grow to approximately 212 billion devices by 2020; a number that includes 30 billion connected devices. IDC sees this growth driven largely by intelligent systems that will be installed and collect data—across both consumer and enterprise applications.

And we're doing all of this connecting on the run. Mobile has freed us from desktops and landlines, and we read, think, react, reach out, share and shop when we want to and wherever we are. Like it or not, this has created a new paradigm—immediacy. The impact is already dramatic, but like the number of users and the degree of interconnection it will grow. Here's why.

In 1998 there were 38 million households with broadband internet. Now 1.2 billion people can access it through their mobile phones. The World Bank says three-quarters of the world is on mobile. That's startling when you consider that it is most often used for social activities and accounts for one in every ten e-dollars spent in the US.

The combination of interconnectivity and mobility changes everything.

We no longer simply go to a company's website to read about their product. In most cases we don't know they exist, and we don't care. Some suggest there are 1.75 billion pages on the internet. If we know the name of a company and its URL (web address), and can be bothered to go straight there, then they'd already be a pretty important brand for us. But we'd still head online to compare their prices and read recent reviews or, more to the point, find out more through social networking via Twitter, LinkedIn or Facebook, which have now overtaken search.

How do we connect?

So how do we find what we want, and what has being in social media got to do with finding it? Mostly we do one of two things:

1   We Google it (or use another search engine).

2   We ask friends.

Our digital footprint dramatically impacts the results of both.

We Google it

When we want something we don't just Google a business name. This is one of the first mistakes many businesses make. They believe we're going to sit down at a desk and type their name into a computer, read what they tell us, believe it, and cough up or turn up.

It simply does not work that way. Now we Google as we think. We're having a coffee, something pops into our mind and we type that into Google: 'Is there really more sugar in yoghurt than ice-cream?'

And because you are different from me and Google knows from previous searches what you like or from your IP address what country you are in, even if we put in the same question we will get different results. Google contextualises our search. This is called personalisation. On the upside, the results are tailored, which is helpful in a noisy world with overwhelming choice. On the downside, this can narrow your view.

Say an elderly parent lands up in hospital one weekend when their health takes an abrupt turn for the worse. We are advised that they will require constant professional medical care. Suddenly we need to find somewhere for them to stay. Do we know if they have a will? Insurance? Who manages their affairs?

An initial search may look something like this:

> Mum sick 82 years needs home 24/7 professional medical care within 25 km Camberwell.

That's if we're thinking straight. We don't plug 'The Wonderful Hospice Company' into Google. We don't know it exists.

And the first company that comes up from this kind of search (called a longtail search because of the length of the question) and is served up on the front page of Google (the only page that counts) is the one we're going to check out.

To get on the front page, that company:

- has a web presence
- has a website optimised for the keywords that people use to search for the services it offers (this is called SEO or search engine optimisation), which is likely to place

'24/7 medical care' (their need) above 'wonderful, caring staff and lovely grounds' (our idea of who we are)

- generates positive recommendations, feedback and conversations in social media networks and the online forums that lead to ratings; social media properties often land on the first page of search results

- puts out good content about their products and services (called content marketing), because this contributes to visibility.

The algorithms that connect you to the information you're looking for take all those elements into account.

You can have the flashiest website in the world but Google is looking for something more: it's trying to pull in real responses from real people because this is what makes your search worthwhile.

And 89 per cent of consumers conduct research using search engines. That makes being a part of those conversations, including managing any complaints that might emerge, very, very important.

Not being there is a problem. Being there if people don't like you is still a problem. So even on the most basic, technical level, being online and engaged has a great impact. But that's just the start.

We ask friends

Here's another reason why participating in social media networks is important. People talk about brands and purchases all the time. And we trust those recommendations.

Personal recommendations have always been important— that's not new. We're far more likely to trust the opinion of someone we know than an anonymous head of marketing.

But what makes those recommendations important is that in other areas trust is on the decline. According to the Edelman Trust Barometer, which has measured trust on a number of dimensions over many years, there's a clear trend. We don't much trust journalists, politicians or CEOs, and over time we have come to trust them less and less.

Although the findings vary, the essence is that we don't trust companies to tell us the truth either. Was this always the case? Possibly, but couple that with the fact that accessibility has taken away the need for gatekeepers and it's clear that the days are gone when you could declare from a position of authority that something was so *because you said it was*.

So who do we trust?

The answer is friends. I am far more likely to go to a café because someone whose opinion I value went there and thought the coffee was good than because of the café's own claims. The interesting thing about trust is that it makes no difference whether the relationship is in a physical or a virtual network. We treat them the same.

The billions of conversations that go on every day in social media networks matter hugely. They influence choices. And the emergence of comparison pricing and rating sites only further entrenches their value. According to econsultancy, 79 per cent of consumers trust online reviews as much as personal recommendations and 73 per cent of consumers say positive customer reviews make them trust a business more. Sixty eight per cent of consumers place greater trust in business with good and bad reviews, and only 12 per cent of consumers say they take no notice of online reviews.

To influence those conversations you have to be in them. You can use social media to acknowledge a mistake or correct misinformation, or to thank someone for a recommendation, further deepening the connection you have with them. While a globally connected world offers choice, it's also overwhelming. If you're where your customers are, listening and responding to their needs, you've created the basis for relationship.

So what is the digital economy?

In a nutshell, the digital economy refers to that part of the economy that is built on the use of digital technologies. But because digital is such an integral part of who we are and the way we do business it's becoming increasingly difficult to disintermediate it from other parts of the economy. Analysts try to do so to show the particular contribution of digital to GDP. This is important because it often provides the evidence business needs to invest.

When you take into account the powerful impact of the internet on behaviour, the significance of the digital economy is much greater than the figures suggest. For example, many people research products online but purchase offline (this is called the ROPO effect). Roughly two-thirds of people use the internet for price discovery. The purchasing decision is a digital experience, but the act of buying takes place in a bricks-and-mortar store because, among other things, people enjoy the social experience of shopping. It is predicted that this effect will continue to grow—a good sign for retailers who are able to strike the right balance in their integrated virtual/real shopping model. According to a new study from the Google Shopper Council in the US, 84 per cent of mobile shoppers use their phones to assist them in their shopping while in physical stores. Shoppers who use mobile services more, spend more in-store. Frequent mobile shoppers spend 25 per cent more in-store than people who only occasionally use a mobile phone to help with shopping.

And what's it worth?

Measuring the value of the digital economy is proof positive that there's more than one way to skin a cat.

I don't want to bombard you with statistics, even though for many executives numbers speak louder than words. I think the late adoption of social technologies is in part due to the fact that information has not been communicated upwards in the right language. A marketer runs excitedly to tell the CEO about a YouTube ad that went viral, and all the CEO can think is, so what? Some of the following facts may help to close that communication gap.

The baseline

According to the International Data Corporation (IDC), the global online economy, including business-to-business (B2B) and business-to-consumer (B2C) ecommerce transactions, was worth US$16 trillion in 2013. (Note that since US dollars are used in almost all the data on social media drawn on in this book, unless otherwise indicated the currency figures refer to US dollars.) Of this, the global market for digital products and services was around $4.4 trillion.

In 2012 the Boston Consulting Group (BCG) published a report predicting that by 2016 online business would contribute $4.2 trillion to the GDP of G20 nations alone, making it the fifth biggest economy worldwide.

Growth

The underlying message in these and other reports is that whatever the current baseline, digital will grow, and grow. Within the economy there will be some interior decorating. For example, in the retail sector online shopping may grow then shrink back as ROPO climbs and retailers stop just broking brands and instead provide shoppers with a high-quality blended service.

Mature markets are expected to grow annually at 8 per cent, but the runaway story is in developing markets where growth is conservatively projected to be twice as fast as in the developed world.

In the UK the digital economy already contributes 8 per cent to GDP, and BCG expects it will contribute an average 5.5 per cent to the GDP of G20 countries by 2016. That provides some countries with a significant advantage over others. For example, Australian digital growth has been only 3.7 per cent compared with the average of 5.5 per cent. This clearly affects productivity.

The BCG report shows that small and medium-sized enterprises that actively engage consumers online have had three-year sales growth rates up to 22 per cent higher than those that don't.

A 2013 three-year joint study by French multinational Capgemini and MIT that surveyed almost 400 firms confirmed this large differential. It showed that businesses that are more digitally mature, the Digirati as the report calls them, have a clear digital advantage over their less mature peers. This trend applies across every industry.

The report found that Digirati:

- were 26 per cent more profitable than their less mature peers

- generated 9 per cent more revenue through their employees and physical assets

- generated 12 per cent higher market valuation ratios.

What distinguishes the Digirati is that they make strategic decisions on where to excel in digital. Their technology-enabled initiatives change their internal operations and engagement with customers, and even transform their business models.

The World Bank believes the adoption of digital technologies can be directly correlated with economic growth. They claim that for every 10 additional mobile phones per 100 people in developing nations GDP grows by 0.8 per cent. Similarly, management consultancy Arthur D. Little found that GDP increases by 1 per cent for every 10 per cent increase in broadband penetration.

Productivity

Social media has frequently been cited as contributing to a time-wasting culture that costs countries billions. This has reinforced a style of leadership in which managers create more processes or systems to grab back 15 minutes a day in productive time from each employee.

In the wrong hands such measures create a focus on inputs rather than outputs, appropriate in a manufacturing environment, for example, but not those based on intellectual capital. They can reflect a mindset based on compliance and control rather than appropriate risk management.

The bigger risk is that they prolong a widget-based leadership mindset that will not equip managers to deal with the complexity required to thrive in the digital and social age.

Many employers continue to ban social media at work, viewing it as a waste of time even though there is a significant body of research to suggest it drives engagement.

It's well recognised, for example, that young professionals value internet-connected mobility over money, and it's the skill set (and mindset) of these digital natives that employers need.

A recent Cisco study found companies that embrace social media during business hours are more attractive to job applicants in the highly competitive talent pool. But it's wrong to think of adopting social networking as a concession to Millennials.

Employees currently spend as much as 20 per cent of their time at work looking for information. McKinsey & Co believe productivity could be increased by as much as 25 per cent by social technologies that increase collaboration. It's a sentiment echoed by professional services multinational Ernst & Young. For one thing, social networking creates searchable content and connections that allow employees to access the right information and people within and across enterprises — fast.

McKinsey Global Institute (MGI) estimates social technology could increase professional productivity by up to 25 per cent. But MGI says that while 72 per cent of companies use social technologies in some way, very few are anywhere near to achieving the full potential benefit, and the most powerful applications of social technologies in the global economy are largely untapped.

Professional services powerhouse Deloitte also believes social technologies will be integral to recruitment and HR. Deloitte itself integrates gamification features such as badges on its top-scoring leader boards at its Deloitte Leadership Academy. Deloitte believes that letting employees share accomplishments on Twitter and LinkedIn is hugely motivating, particularly in a world where it's critical to maintain a personal brand. A caveat here is that a trusted personal brand does not mean just pushing personal strengths. As author and co-chairman of Deloitte's Center for the Edge John Hagel says, sharing a more complete picture of who we are, including vulnerabilities and weaknesses, is critical for creating trust. Likewise CMO of Extreme Networks and Huffington Post columnist Vala Afshar says that authentic leadership is an important characteristic of building social influence.

Interestingly, employee wellbeing is typically high on the list of factors believed to increase individual productivity, but the role of social media in driving engagement has not, to my knowledge, been directly investigated.

Going forward, productivity measures will need to take into account the impacts of the connected 'digital and social ecosystem' on motivation, which are not easy to quantify.

The value of digital to productivity means measuring direct contributions from pure online businesses but also the indirect activity of mixed businesses, including the use of social media for engagement, sales and customer service. This is a paradigm shift that demands a change in the mindset of business leaders that starts with recognising that in a hyper-connected world, connectivity itself is an enabler and a multiplier.

Shopping

Here's another reason having a social media presence matters: *people online are shopping.* And there's hard data that the research they do in social networks influences what they buy.

Although social networks influence decision-making on- and offline (who people vote for, say, or what accountant they use), consider that this year ecommerce is growing at a staggering 20 per cent.

Ecommerce over Thanksgiving in the US in 2012 rose 26 per cent from the year before to $1.042 billion, the highest revenue generator being the online store Amazon. This was modest compared with the $3 billion Chinese consumers spent in 24 hours on China's equivalent online marketplace, Taobao.

According to Nielsen, 70 per cent of active online adult social networkers shop online and 53 per cent follow a brand. The internet marketing news organ *Marketing Land* tells us that 91 per cent of people have gone into a store because of an online experience; and 62 per cent of consumers end up making a purchase in-store after researching it online. This is the ROPO phenomenon mentioned earlier. But it's only going to be a business benefit if your website and social media ecosystem create that opportunity.

Forbes writer Steve Olenski notes that 78 per cent of consumers claim the posts made by companies on social media influence their purchases, or as high as 81 per cent if the comments are from friends in social networks.

Small to medium-sized enterprises (SMEs) lag behind better-resourced organisations such as the *Fortune* 100s, which have taken these trends to heart:

- 87 per cent of *Fortune* 100 companies use social media
- 75 per cent of *Fortune* 100 companies are on Facebook
- 73 per cent of *Fortune* 500 companies have a Twitter account
- 66 per cent of *Fortune* 500 companies have a Facebook page
- their corporate YouTube channels average two million views
- *Fortune* 100 companies have multiple accounts per region (one size does not fit all, and culture counts)
- 50 per cent of *Fortune* 100 companies have a Google Plus account
- 25 per cent are on Pinterest.

Depending on where you look, SMEs come in around the 30 per cent level. SMEs face a number of barriers, ranging from lack of time and resourcing to a lack of understanding of social media.

Of those that are in social media, many whack up a Facebook page or start a Twitter feed because they believe they 'should', instead of asking the deeper, age-old questions about who they are as a business, why they are there and what their customers want—in other words, having a strategy.

A disconnect is that many leaders continue to think about social media as a channel specifically for communications or sales. But its reach is far greater. What social media, like technology, delivers is an expectation that cannot necessarily be delivered under legacy business structures: *immediacy*.

This can in part be addressed at a channel level, for example by adapting websites for mobile to generate sales by suggesting additional options at the point of sale. (Not surprisingly, those customers want issues resolved just as fast and in an online space that suits them.) But there's increasing evidence that this is not enough and that it's the companies that 'get' digital as a 'way of being' rather than farming it out to the marketing department that outperform their peers.

In his excellent article 'The Operating Model That Is Eating the World', the CEO of Undercurrent, Aaron Dignan, suggests those businesses that are structured to respond quickly to changing needs are the ones that will thrive. He cites numerous examples of businesses built on little capital but big ideas that grow into multi-million-dollar markets (software companies Medium, Hipchat, Circa, Outbox and Quirky through to giants like Amazon, Google, Twitter, Facebook and PayPal) that dominate the online sphere.

They have in common the same intensely customer-focused model with its bias to action is increasingly (and successfully) being adopted by businesses that sell physical products and services 'in real life'. What differentiates them is that like their forbears in the software industry they are nimble and are able to tap into (or create) customer demand and collaborate with future users, giving the product wings.

Amazon is a global marketplace. Facebook and Google are effective online advertising companies. They understand the power of digital in its entirety and in particular how cloud, mobile and social computing and predictive analysis together can produce massive competitive advantage.

Categories like real estate or car services (compare Uber with conventional taxi services) look increasingly like technology platforms where product is the equivalent of inventory and the core business value is 'in the data, the tools and the optimisation of markets'.

Companies with lower capital and operating costs and more flexible and intelligent systems and platforms can be a huge threat.

Future growth

And there is still plenty of space for newcomers. According to Professor Panko Ghemawat at IESE Business School and author of *World 3.0*, the extent to which we are globalised has been overstated. Ghemawat argues that the world is only semi-globalised, leaving plenty of room for growth and improvement in global welfare.

For example in education, while international students are found on campuses across the world, only 2 per cent of university students are studying in countries where they are not citizens. On the investment front, in 2010 less than 10 per cent were a result of direct foreign investments. Even on Facebook, which is a truly global platform, Ghemawat says that only 10 to 15 per cent of Facebook friends are from another country.

This suggests one thing — opportunity.

Digital literacy is the new financial literacy

Finally, executives have to get social because they need to be able to speak the language of the connected world. While corporate disasters have led to increased demand for governance and financial literacy at the uppermost leadership levels, we are not yet demanding the same of arguably the biggest game changer of all, technology.

Although a lack of understanding of digital may not lead to fraud, it can expose the organisation to brand damage or loss of competitiveness with equally harsh results.

Putting aside its life-changing impacts on everything from the way we meet to the way we connect and collaborate, the figures alone tell a tale. In 2013 IT research firm Gartner showed that worldwide ICT spend surpassed $3.7 trillion. That includes IT (hardware and software), digital (the content layer) and social (the way technology allows people to connect).

Clearly, leaders need to understand what outcomes they can expect from this level of investment. Specifically:

1   How will data translate into useful knowledge and be used for business outcomes?

2   How will cloud impact traditional models of procurement?

3   Can social media be used strategically and what is the ROI?

While social platforms do not carry the same costs as infrastructure, concerns about their value remain. But it's not just about the money.

The power of social media to organise and influence played out in 2012 through the London riots, the Arab Spring and recently in the US elections, where online campaign spending rose 616 per cent compared with 2008 and played a tangible role in the outcome.

Despite this, there is a glaring lack of digital literacy at the top. But leaders are not alone, with many IT professionals unable to fully understand social in the strategic sense. In a recent Capgemini study, over 90 per cent of companies stated that they did not have the necessary social media skills.

How can boards sign off on the company's strategy and marketing plan without understanding the social media component, or in some cases the lack of one? And what should CEOs, in turn, be demanding of their teams?

C-suites seem yet to fully grasp the direct business implications of digital change. One reason for this is the perception of digital as a support function rather than as central to leadership. Many leaders acquired their power in a pre-internet world and are finding it difficult to deal with digital issues and unsure how to bridge the gap.

Digital literacy is a skill, and like any skill it can be learned. In a connected world leaders must know how to assess the opportunities and risks of digital on their business without being technocrats.

Forrester Research predicts that by 2016 half of all dollars spent online will be influenced by the web, which creates a great opportunity for leaders who know how to leverage it and a risk for those who don't. Digital and social literacy are must-have future skills.

The social media statistical zoo

It's a zoo out there when it comes to social media metrics. I could have drawn on any thousands of those available, but here are just a few to give you a sense of the lay of the land:

- Twitter has over 100 million daily active users, of which 75 per cent are on mobile. (*Social Media Today*)
- 63 per cent of brands have multiple Twitter accounts. (Mashable)
- 55 per cent of recruiters use Twitter to find and vet potential candidates. (All Twitter)
- LinkedIn has 259 million users. (CNET)
- There are 3 million LinkedIn company pages connecting 225 million professionals on the network. (LinkedIn)

(continued)

The social media statistical zoo *(cont'd)*

- LinkedIn is used as a talent solution by 91 of the *Fortune* 100 companies. (LinkedIn)

- SlideShare has 50 million active users and gets 159 million page views a month; 1.4 million other websites have embedded SlideShare presentations and 1 billion slides are viewed monthly on other properties. (SlideShare)

- There are now over 343 million active users on Google Plus. (http://www.zdnet.com/)

- 67 per cent of US internet users and 82 per cent of UK internet users are on Facebook. (Business Insider)

- 78 per cent of US Facebook users are mobile. (TechCrunch)

- 16 million small businesses actively used Facebook pages in 2013. (Small Biz Trends)

- 52 per cent of all marketers generated a lead from Facebook this year. (HubSpot)

- Of the *Fortune* 500 companies in the United States, 22.4 per cent have active Instagram accounts. (Buffer)

- The most photographed brand on Instagram is Nike with over 19 million posts mentioning the Nike hashtag and adding over one million more mentions monthly. (Nitrogram)

Chapter summary

The data clearly shows that the digital economy is gargantuan and growing. The shift:

- represents a structural change

- impacts the whole economy

- applies across every area of business, not just marketing or sales

- impacts productivity and the bottom line.

You've got to be in it to win it. And the first step is to get your mind in the game.

CHAPTER 2

Six damaging myths about social media

So why, given the compelling data on the business value of social media, are executives missing in action? Because they are anchored to damaging myths about social media that are holding them back. And here are six of them.

1 Social media is a fad.

2 Social media is for posting photos of what you ate for lunch.

3 Social media is for code monkeys.

4 Social media is for people under 25.

5 Social media is for marketing.

6 There's no ROI on social media.

The eruption of social media seemed to happen so fast and was so visibly associated with teen geekery that an inaccurate but influential narrative took hold.

What springs to mind when someone mentions Facebook? Distraction, time-wasting, cyberbullying, Millennials? It's rarely 'global customer growth strategy', 'targeted advertising' or 'real-time customer support'. LinkedIn? Isn't that the place where people post their CVs? Not really.

However, these myths are pervasive and have generated an anti-social mindset. Here are some of the truths behind them.

Myth #1: Social media is a fad

It's hard to raise 'social media' at an executive event without at least a handful of people dismissing it as a wasteful fad. Of all the myths, this is probably the most strongly held. It is also wrong.

For example, LinkedIn, the professional social networking site, was founded in 2002. LinkedIn now has 260 million users in more than 200 countries and is available in 20 different languages for people to network, recruit, raise equity, market their companies or share expertise through various channels, including groups. And that's just the start.

When people think of Facebook, they tend to think of the college kid Mark Zuckerberg. But Facebook is over a decade old. As for Zuckerberg, that 'kid' is now a 30-year old billionaire CEO leading 6000 employees of a listed company worth about $100 billion and earning about $3 billion per quarter. Facebook is a sophisticated business and one of the few to have built agility and strategy into the heart of the business through cloud, social and mobile computing, and predictive analysis.

YouTube? This video-sharing website started in 2005. (It was not the first social video-sharing site: Metacafe was established in 2003 and Vimeo followed in 2004.) More than a billion people visit each month, watching around six billion hours of video. When I first decided to post an education campaign to YouTube in 2008, I remember being told by an advertising agency that it would never work because YouTube was for entertainment, not information. Now the YouTube education channel has tens of millions of subscribers worldwide. YouTube EDU provides access to teachers, short lessons and full courses from the world's leading universities.

A relative newcomer, the microblog Twitter has been around since 2006. Twitter now handles 500 million tweets and 1.6 billion search queries *every day*.

And as those in the know will tell you, there were many precursors to these giants dating back to the nineties (Friendster, for example) and earlier. What's more, the platforms are continuing to grow and are becoming increasingly sophisticated in response to user demand. There are now literally hundreds of social media platforms, and more are springing up every day. This is contributing to a sense of overwhelm, especially among newcomers. You don't need to know about most of them, though, and you certainly don't need to use them all.

It is important, however, to be aware of the well-established platforms and what they do. These include:

- Twitter
- LinkedIn
- SlideShare
- Facebook
- Google Plus
- YouTube, Instagram and Pinterest.

As all these will contribute to your Professional Platform, we will examine them later in detail. Here we need only underline the point that social media is not a fad. It is here to stay and we all need to know how to use it.

Truth: Social media is at least 12 years old and is growing strongly.

Myth #2: Social media is about posting photos of what you ate for lunch

Take a quick look at Instagram or Facebook and it's no surprise that people think social media is about posting photos of what you ate for lunch. The data certainly supports an obsession with taking and sharing photos and videos around the world.

There are literally hundreds of photo-sharing sites, such as Flickr, Zooomr, Picasa and Photobucket. The more popular video-sharing sites include Viddler, Vimeo, Dailymotion, Facebook, YouTube, Ustream, Blip.tv, Qik, Metacafe, Break and Veoh, although again the full list runs to the hundreds.

Social media platforms are also integrating video and photo sharing functionality. For example, last year Twitter introduced a mobile app called The Vine that allows users to create short videos of up to six seconds; Instagram offers fifteen seconds.

And we are creating a lot of them:

- Snapchat (which deletes photos once they are viewed) — 400 million/day

- Instagram — 50 million/day

- Facebook — 350 million/day

- YouTube — 100 hours of video uploaded every minute (you do the maths).

In 2013 'selfie', used to describe a photo taken of yourself and posted on social media, was named word of the year by the *Oxford Dictionary*'s editors after the frequency of its usage increased by 17 000 per cent in a year.

So there's no denying that posting photos is integral to social media. But I want to put it in context. Imagine you've been in a four-hour board meeting and you break for lunch. Someone brings in a tray of sandwiches and you turn to a colleague and say, 'Oh, chicken sandwiches. I love them'.

This comment is totally within context, it's appropriate and reveals something of your human self. Such revelations are vital for building strong, connected business relationships. But they are not what the four-hour meeting was about.

Photos in social media are, similarly, a record of a moment in time: *I was here. This is what caught my attention*. The difference is that the chicken sandwich remark instantly evaporates into the ether, never to be heard of again. Not so in social media, or at least the kind of social media we've been using to date, where everything we share is published and remains online for good. Even this, however, is now changing.

Snapchat, for example, is a photo messaging app that allows users to share photos, videos, text and drawings — but with a difference. First, content is shared with a controlled list and, second, you can set a time limit for how long they can be viewed (1–10 seconds). After that, content is hidden from the recipient's device and deleted from Snapchat's servers.

The exodus of teenagers from Facebook to Snapchat suggests that this privacy feature is highly valued. Facebook is being widely sued for breaching user privacy, and given an alternative, users are voting with their, er, fingers.

But the Snapchat migration only reinforces the message that users are not looking to leave the social media ecosystem, but simply to find better alternatives within it, of which there are likely to be many as social media continues to mature.

There are also enormous business benefits, in particular for visual brands, in using video- and photo-sharing social media, which I discuss later on. In the meantime, it's good to put the chicken sandwich in context.

Truth: Social media captures human moments.

Myth #3: Social media is for code monkeys

Social media is not about technology and it's not about the tools. It's about what these tools allow you to do, and that's the oldest thing in the world—building relationships.

Yes these platforms have to be built and yes people who know how to code build them. But you don't need to know about that, any more than you had to learn to build electronic circuits in order to watch TV. (I will make a point later on the importance of 'codeability', rather than specific codes, in a digital world.)

Nonetheless, these ideas have become first confused, then linked, then mythologised so that 'social media' elicits images of bleary-eyed students in tracksuits doing all-night hacks... and all the other stereotypes relating to code monkeys.

Why bark if you have a dog? Sure, it's an icky business idiom, but it makes the critical point that knowing how to do something is not as important as knowing how to do something about it. As far back as 2007 award-winning author and principal analyst at Altimeter Group, Brian Solis, wrote that social media was about sociology, not technology.

> Technology is just that, technology. The tools will change. The networks will evolve. Mediums for distributing content will grow. Along with it, behavior will too continue to adapt. In the era of the attention crash and social network fatigue, it is absolutely critical that we step back to realize that we are the communication bridge between companies and people. However, we also must realize that in the era of social media, people also have amplified voices and are now a powerful channel of peer-to-peer influence—for better or for worse.

This nicely captures the importance, and unimportance, of social media tools. And as to creating relationships and connections, building trust and exchanging value—these are things executives know a lot about.

To stay relevant you need to:

- extend your existing connections into social networks, where your customers and suppliers, and your existing and future employees already are.

- reach out to people from all over the world who you do not yet know and activate the many latent and mutually beneficial relationships. The algorithms built into social media networks will help you to find them. That's the only part that requires code. And you do not have to write it.

Truth: Social media is about relationships.

Myth #4: Social media is for people under 25

In many ways this is an extension of the previous myth, and it's absolutely not borne out by the data. As we've already noted, eight new people come online every second. Are all these people 25 and under? Not even close.

With the exception of executives, people from all age groups are becoming more confident about global platforms and are flocking to them. For example, on LinkedIn, which is specifically for professionals, two new people join every second. On Twitter the fastest-growing demographic in 2013 was adults aged 55–65, with a jump of 70 per cent; for Facebook those aged 55–65 jumped 46 per cent in the same time frame, and Google Plus users increased around 57 per cent.

Doing social does not mean you have to start speaking 'lol' or 'awesome'. Authenticity is encouraged and valued. That doesn't mean you should say uncensored what you feel about all issues. Just as in real life, you take the measure of a situation and make judgement calls about when and how to respond, when to hold back, when to share and when to be more reticent. But the days of pre-scripted corporate speak that makes you sound more like a bot than the bots do are, thankfully, fading fast.

Truth: Social media is for everyone.

Myth #5: Social media is for marketing

Yes most marketers are using social media—some poorly, some well—but social media is about a lot more than marketing. With social media, the endgame is to socialise the business, creating connection through every layer of business structure and every level of the business cycle. That means social CEOs, social C-suites, social customer service, social sales, social research.

Because marketers were some of the first to see the potential of social media and because they are creative and experimental, many hopped in to try it out. Unfortunately this association of marketing with social media puts executives off, because many do not believe marketing demonstrates a rigorous return on investment (ROI).

A 2011 study of 600 CEOs showed 73 per cent thought marketing lacked business credibility and were tired of being asked for money without a forecasted business impact. In the past it has always been more difficult for marketing to measure direct and indirect impacts and ROI. (I will get to that in more detail in a moment. Here I'll simply say that is not as big a problem these days.) Yet, not surprisingly, very few companies are willing to give up their marketing activities. The value may not be as easy to measure as a direct transaction, but executives do understand this value.

The problem is that many leaders continue to think about social media as a channel, specifically for communications or sales. But its reach is far greater. What social media, like technology, delivers is an expectation that cannot necessarily be delivered under legacy business structures—immediacy.

This can in part be addressed at the channel level. For example, many social media users shop by smartphone, and businesses that have successfully adapted to mobile can generate sales by suggesting additional options at the point of sale. (Not surprisingly, those customers want issues resolved just as fast, and in an online space that suits them.) But there's increasing evidence that this is not enough and that it's the companies that 'get' digital as a 'way of being' rather than a 'handball-to-marketing' that outperform their peers.

Several studies show that the real business benefits of digital emerge as a result of this deep structural transformation and not fashion-driven tinkering at the edges. A view that social media is marketing is first generation thinking; we are beyond that now, using social to drive transformation across the business.

Truth: Social media is about immediacy and connectivity, and impacts the whole of business.

Myth #6: There's no ROI on social media

The *Harvard Business Review* finds one of the toughest challenges for executives is tying social investments to the bottom line and linking social media efforts to ROI.

Metrics are becoming more sophisticated, however. There are increasingly cloud-based data analytics engines that can merge all sources of data across all channels to deliver credible ROI reports. Many social media metrics companies offer products that allow businesses to enter consumers' social media ecosystem and to track with absolute precision what they click, where they land, how much time they spend there and whether that activity translates into a sale. Even if a user does not purchase something at that time, if they later return to do so, that can be tracked. Ironically, this newfound ability to account for every click of the customer journey is backfiring as consumers become more concerned about privacy and are acting to protect their online activities by using anonymous search functions such as DuckDuckGo.

Meanwhile the question remains: is there any way to calculate the return on investment (ROI) of social media versus other channels?

While there are numerous metrics that make that promise, the short and disappointing answer is not easily, or at least not definitively. The difficulty of distinguishing the buying context—such as via ecommerce advertising or social media recommendations—means there is not yet a conclusive measure for the contribution of social engagement overall. However, there are some effective ways to make an evaluation.

The most advanced tools capture the non-financial value of lead indicators, such as online relationships. Since word-of-mouth recommendations are one of the cheapest and most effective forms of marketing, getting some background on how online relationships influence the purchasing decisions of consumers is a useful exercise for business leaders.

In this case, the return on investment of social media could be measured by the cost saving from trying to obtain the same data by other means, such as through focus groups, which are expensive, or surveys, which can be unreliable.

For example, a recent report by Forrester Research argues that an effective social media marketing scorecard considers metrics from four different perspectives:

1 *Financial:* Has revenue or profit increased, or have costs decreased?

2 *Brand:* Have consumer attitudes about the brand improved?

3   *Risk management:* Is the organisation better prepared to note and respond to attacks or problems that affect reputation?

4   *Digital:* Has the company enhanced its digital assets?

Forrester quotes computer company Dell Outlet's Twitter account as having 'generated millions for Dell'. Dell claims it generates sales from its Twitter accounts by 'posting offers and responding to questions', although the details are sketchy. Dell's in-house marketing manager, Stephanie Nelson, wrote that the company had earned $2 million in two years (2007–2009) when people followed links from Twitter to the Dell Outlet site. She says it also created interest in new products, although there is no measure of the return from this interest in the form of sales.

Using a different measure, computer chip maker Intel says its blog for partners Channel Voice has decreased costs by eliminating the need for expensive in-person events.

Procter & Gamble used media mix modelling, which analyses sales data to determine the effectiveness of the marketing mix, to demonstrate that the community of teenage girl–oriented advice site Beinggirl.com is several times more effective at driving sales of its feminine hygiene products than its television ads.

These results underscore the value of social relationships as indicators of future sales, even though the exact engagement-to-sale trajectory is not mapped.

The dilemma for leaders is that these social relationships are powerful, whether or not their company chooses to participate in them. From the start of the internet, people began sharing shopping experiences and recommending or criticising brands just as they would in conversation.

The worldwide decline in trust towards institutions meant people stopped believing what companies had to say about themselves some decades ago. Instead, the rise of peer-to-peer trust (which is still growing) meant recommendations from friends started having a broader reach than in the past.

A 2011 IBM study shows consumers creating as much information every two days as they did in the period from the dawn of civilisation to 2003. Those recommendations were being made in social networks where corporates were noticeably absent — at least initially.

A simple search will provide companies with detailed consumer sentiment and trend data that allows them to track what keywords are used to find products and which of those lead to sales. Strategies can be refined accordingly.

Data mining is another option: it allows businesses to compare comments on products by different providers and aggregate these with ratings and reviews to better understand what customers want and how their competitors are faring.

Location-based data also allows businesses to pinpoint where conversations about their products are happening and to identify potential new markets; growth in these areas would provide further financial measures.

Another powerful tool is data-driven web optimisation, which allows data to be tested, analysed and measured. For example, market research company eMarketer improved its subscription conversion rate by 53 per cent by removing the price from the description after reviewing data that showed reader preferences. It is possible to measure what it costs to get this benefit against achieving the same results by conventional means.

Online feedback on products also allows companies to quickly refine their offering or approach. Leading Company reports how one financial services company increased lead generation by 40 per cent through better design and by delivering content that focused on the benefits of the product while reducing non-essential information as a result of information it had received directly by engaging customers across multiple platforms.

In all these examples acquiring data by other techniques, including using large teams to cold-call clients, can be expensive. The cost saving could be used as part of the ROI measure of the project.

As far as campaigns are concerned it's possible to track the journey of a customer from click to click, although this tells us more about the influence of a specific campaign than about the factors that influenced the lead-up to a decision.

However, we do know that engaged communities lead to sales down the line. American health and nutrition retail company GNC is an example of a store that built online communities interested in health and provided experts to answer questions at no cost, and without directly chasing sales. This initiative created a 'halo effect' of positive sentiment that ultimately helped anchor people to the brand and converted to sales over time.

Because B2B is immersed in the same social and mobile ecosystem as customers, suppliers and competitors, the need to create positive impressions online is just as critical, perhaps more so, since 60 per cent of the buying circle is over before a prospect makes contact.

Research shows top social adopters like IBM, DELL, Intel and Microsoft 'get' digital as a business tool and use it effectively, not because they are IT companies either.

B2B companies have much to gain by providing value to prospects and they can do this by generating useful content such as ebooks. Creating offers that prospects can act on is an effective way to generate leads that can be measured. And while existing B2Bs have made a slower transition into the social space than consumer brands, given the rise in participation globally their involvement is inevitable.

Peer-to-peer conversations influence behavior, and in an environment in which these relationships are more trusted than anything else, businesses must take notice of them, even in the absence of a perfect measure of ROI for all aspects of social media.

But ROI is far broader than all of the above. How, for example, do we measure the value of a relationship?

Having said all this, in 2013 *Business Insider* reported that many brands were moving away from metrics that purported to measure social media ROI because they recognised that social media was not a transactional action and that indicators, for example on financial returns, showed secondary effects. The trend is not universal, however, as many social commerce applications and direct response campaigns are able to show measurable effects using social media networks.

BI reported that between 2010 and 2013 the proportion of marketers using a revenue-per-customer metric on social media fell from 17 to 9 per cent, according to the February 2013 CMO survey. The percentage tracking conversion rates also dropped, from 25 to 21 per cent.

The focus has shifted to measures that reflect audience building, brand awareness and customer relations through metrics such as reach, engagement and sentiment, all subjects of this book.

The General Manager from Kinship Digital, Walter Adamson, says the discussion on social media ROI should be qualified to external social media networks because enterprise social networks across businesses yield significant ROI when done properly. However, Gartner is well quoted as saying that 80 per cent of enterprise social networks fail to meet their objectives during implementation, often because of poor analysis or strategy.

Truth: ROI is complex to measure, but social and digital deliver measurable value.

Chapter summary

Here are six truths about social media.

1   Social media is at least 12 years old and growing strongly.

2   Social media captures human moments.

3   Social media is about relationships.

4   Social media is for everyone.

5   Social media is about immediacy and connectivity, and impacts the whole of business.

6   ROI is complex to measure, but social and digital deliver measurable value. There are many, however, who believe you need to be in social to understand it. I am one of them.

CHAPTER 3

Mindshift: from 'so what' to 'social'

Exposing the myths about social media is helpful but we also have to look at how factors in the broader environment contribute to an anti-social mindset. These factors include:

- traditional business practices
- the unprecedented, accelerating speed of change
- high uncertainty and ambiguity
- fear.

Traditional business practices

Executives make data-driven investment decisions and manage risk. Ironically these qualities, vital for success, are the same ones that have kept them out of social media.

The way we do business

An example is data-driven strategy. While traditionally this approach has given companies a strategic edge, the kind of business intelligence required to back moves into social media was simply not available when social media first erupted. It was a place where people went to talk to other people. Who needed to measure that? Of course, we forgot that people speaking to people pretty much underpins everything that happens in life. And social media grew fast. By the time business had recognised this, the horse had already bolted.

First movers took leaps in the dark and learned as they went along; some soared and at times some crashed. We all learned from the early adopters. Not all organisations, however, are suited or open to experimenting. The location, size, infrastructure, risk appetite, culture and leadership of a company all influence how willingly it will embrace change and how quickly it is capable of adjusting.

What well-established, large and often effective business systems deliver in strength can be offset by a lack of agility. Often we see assets become liabilities when business dynamics change.

Timing

Although there is no evidence specifically examining the link between post-GFC conditions and the uptake of social media, the economic climate must have had an impact. Social media experienced burgeoning growth at a time when many businesses were treading water to stay afloat. For many the possible benefits of new technologies were not adequately offset by its unknown risks in an environment that had become suddenly and strongly risk adverse. Instead of finding ways to innovate out of the doldrums, many retreated to the tried and true.

Traditional structures

In the past the many different areas of a business were able to operate in relative isolation. This was never ideal. One big leadership challenge has always been to ensure different areas of the business are talking to one another. But it was possible for a chief information officer (CIO) to run out a computer refresh without needing the approval of the chief marketing officer (CMO). Nowadays where marketing is automated and IT-dependent such a move would be a disaster.

Senior leaders failed to understand the difference between IT, digital and social media influences. Many businesses did not (and still do not) understand that social media platforms are not $100 million IT investments. Indeed, many are free. They do, however, require people to manage them, and online engagement is human resource intense.

Having said that, social media efforts cannot work long term in isolation from deeper business and market transformation. Adopting social media at the enterprise level requires technical analysis and investment and also a deep rethink on how business areas are structured.

However, change does not have to follow an all-or-nothing approach. Organisations can experiment with pilot projects and learn from their users what works. Consultancies are right in pointing out that a deep digital transformation creates the best results, but this idea can put off small or medium-sized businesses who desperately need to get into the space. They think, wrongly, that it means either a multi-million-dollar investment or nothing, whereas mostly it's a continuum.

The old guard

The difference in the level of awareness among senior decision-makers also influences how willing organisations are to become social. This is at every level across the C-suite and includes legal, customer service and sales officers. Organisations that moved early to adopt digital and social technologies often claim to have had passionate internal champions who were able to socialise new ideas. A culture has to be open to change or the old guard becomes entrenched. There's nothing wrong with the old guard, but we need to be willing to extend our ideas.

CIOs are a case in point, although I do not want to limit my observations to them. Leading CIOs foresaw the potential of social media years ago and have been instrumental in raising awareness about its impacts. They also recognise their skills will increasingly converge with those of marketers who rely heavily on IT systems. Others, possibly out of fear of diminishing authority or just a lack of awareness, actively spoke against it, not because they understood the risks or opportunities of social business but because they did not understand what it was. This is like the initial reaction to cloud computing. Leaders need to acknowledge these reactions and not be limited by them. Seek out alternative views. Go beyond the boundaries of your organisation.

One way they did this was to use (some might say 'abuse') their technological expertise to scare executives. Using jargon and tightly held expert knowledge to control business direction is nothing new and is certainly not restricted to technology. But I know many innovators who have been thwarted by internal processes, for example where IT demands the same business case (complete with Project Governance Boards) for an online consultation pilot as for a $100 million IT project. While absolutely appropriate in some cases, when misapplied this kind of oversight kills new ideas. Applying a one-size-fits-all governance approach to a project because it mentions technology is rigidity, not good governance. Leaders have to weigh up risk, including the risks of absence, and apply the right governance model. The same could be said for change management, where calls for detailed change management plans and teams derail opportunities to get started in social. Social technologies can be a real threat to that because they give people the power to manage change themselves.

It's no different in marketing, though, where old-school executives are still bidding for traditional branding and advertising campaign money, and believe that because the media spend includes online advertising they have ticked the social box.

Traditionally executives relied on internal subject matter experts to bring credible research and new ideas to the executive table. But if these subject matter experts are themselves afraid and out of touch, how does it get there?

I think executives in the current environment would be mad to assume even their most trusted colleagues understand what is happening. They should be challenging their direct reports by asking these questions:

- What game-changing technologies could blow our business out of the water?

- Who is lurking on the perimeter of our business and capable of shaving two or three per cent off our revenue for themselves?

- What impact could technology have on our business area?

- What are we doing to leverage the opportunities new technologies could deliver to our business area?

- What are we doing to manage the risk?

Only by embedding performance outcomes will the tide of laziness shift.

Analysis paralysis

The idea that social technologies are an entertainment craze for the young has died. Instead, research is continuing to point to online connectivity as a business advantage.

However, despite hundreds of studies by highly reputable research and advisory firms that point to the benefits of social business, the needle for executive engagement has barely moved. Executives frequently cite a lack of research or proven business case as a reason for not engaging. But when you ask if they've read any reports on the value of social media, the more honest among them will admit that they have not.

Although there are probably millions of anecdotes about the transformative impact of social media, there is a growing foundation of solid research too.

For example, in 2013 an MIT, *Sloan Management Review* and Deloitte social business study of 2545 respondents from 25 industries and 99 countries found that not only had awareness of the importance of social business for today and tomorrow risen steeply, but it had done so across every industry. The report found that companies deliberately nurturing a more social culture understood the importance of executive involvement. Even though social ROI measures are still evolving, these companies are already investing in quality content marketing and refining their business approach as they go along and as more business intelligence becomes available.

This does not mean social technologies are a business panacea. Businesses have to deal with massive complexities, including many outside their control such as the political environment and other factors that impact productivity.

Furthermore, technology creates solutions but in doing so reveals new problems. This is evident in the decline of the number of unskilled roles compared with those in emerging digital industries. But this cyclical process of adapting and innovating in response to change in the internal and external environment is not new. What has changed is the speed at which it is happening. And that is a key challenge.

The unprecedented, accelerating speed of change

Few could have predicted the speed at which new technologies would take hold or how pervasive their impact would be. We are living in a time when more information is created in a day than a village of people once acquired over a lifetime, when the lead of a new product is snatched away even while it waits for a patent to be approved, and when we leap towards a technology that takes us to the edge of our comfort zone only to discover it's already obsolete.

We respond somewhere on the continuum of:

- feeling overwhelmed and freezing, doing nothing, which comes at a high cost (likely to become apparent later rather than now); or

- chasing our tails by trying to keep up, which is impossible and keeps us distracted rather than focused on developing the right strategy using the right technologies for our particular business.

We had better get used to it, though, because the speed of change is not going to slow. Rather, because (to use Toffler's phrase) 'technology makes more technology possible', it will speed up.

According to futurists such as Ray Kurzweil, in the next hundred years we will experience the equivalent of 20 000 years' worth of change. Change used to be linear, or even evolutionary, one shift enabling the next. But if Kurzweil and others are correct, we are moving towards a time when we will be in a state of almost constant paradigmatic shift. The nature of change has itself changed. It has become exponential.

What does this mean for business? It has to be structured to respond to immediacy.

Snapchat is a great example of a company that was able to identify and respond to an issue that is touching a nerve for people around the world—privacy.

From revelations that security organisations are spying on citizens to suggestions that social media companies are scanning people's private conversations, people feel exposed, even betrayed. They want to be social but they also want to be private. Some argue that if you have nothing to hide, privacy is not an issue. That's like suggesting there's no need for doors on public bathrooms or that we should be willing to share every part of our lives. This is not true. Segmenting what we share is appropriate. That we have survived cancer may not be something we want a future employer to know. It might bias them (even unconsciously) in ways that disadvantage us. If we're a trauma coach, however, it might be a message we *want* widely shared. Or we might want to work through a fight we had with our spouse by talking it over with a close friend, but not the general public.

In December 2012 the photo-sharing giant Instagram changed its terms and conditions. People interpreted the change to mean that their content could be used in advertising and other ways they hadn't anticipated. 'Instascam', as it was labelled, created so much outrage that Instagram was forced to clarify its position. The company gave people a stark choice: take it or leave it, because they could. The doggedness that comes from being a virtual monopoly power doesn't change because a company is in social media rather than consumer goods. People weren't happy and many left, but the user base is so large that it hardly made a dent. At least, that day.

Things have since changed. Understanding many people's preference for privacy, Snapchat allows users to exchange photos but deletes them as soon as they're viewed, including off the Snapchat server. There has been an exodus, particularly among teens, from Facebook and Instagram. In December 2012 Snapchat had 50 million users; now it has 200 million. And as the social media environment continues to evolve, there will be no shortage of alternatives going forward.

Immediacy, immediacy, immediacy. A business that can evolve quickly can leverage opportunity.

Business has to reconsider everything from IT infrastructure (making sure it's accessible to the increasing number of people wanting to transact on mobile while they're on the move) to migrating customer service to social media platforms or even crowdsourcing their business intelligence. These are significant issues but not ones that can be avoided by pretending they do not or will not pose a threat to the way we now do business.

High uncertainty and ambiguity

The accelerating speed of change is creating high uncertainty in every area, with an inevitable flow-on to business. For example, before a business can crowdsource recommendations from avid fans, it has to know that is acceptable under the laws and regulations that govern its business. What's a go in consumer goods may, for example, be illegal in finance.

Unfortunately, many regulators are no more progressed in knowing how to respond to this unprecedented change than business. Many dismissed social technologies as a flash in the pan and failed to plan proactively for the massive consequences of their growth. A good example of the impact of online conversations on the buying cycle can be found in the area of consumer law.

Many of the searches made every day on browsers like Google are by consumers researching and comparing products. Consumers also seek the recommendations of friends both in real life and on virtual networks. These recommendations are more important than traditional marketing because we tend to trust the opinions of friends above those of companies, which we expect to feed us spin. Not surprisingly, some companies have tried to exploit this trend and are paying people, either directly or by using incentives, to write product reviews. Depending on where you live, this is often illegal.

Spam is another legal minefield. More than 100 billion spam emails are sent daily. It's one thing to send spam on purpose, another to do it without even realising you are breaking the law. In Australia, for example, you need the express consent of someone to contact them using their email. That means if they subscribe to your company site for safety information you can't send them an offer for cosmetics, even though they have willingly given you their contact details. Many marketers think they can use the names in their database however they like, which is not the case.

The impact of technology on business goes way beyond social media and can be seen in the explosion of issues relating to copyright, defamation and media law, privacy and security, technology, telecommunications, trademark and brand protection, and social media law.

Interestingly as I was writing this book, the first Australian Twitter defamation battle proceeded to a full trial and a teacher made legal history after a former student was ordered to pay AU$105 000 for defaming her on Twitter and Facebook.

Fear

We have to tell it like it is: a key reason executives stay away from social media is fear. And that's also why a lot of them denigrate it. This continues an age-old tradition of diminishing the importance of something because we don't understand it. Fortunately, being adaptable is also an age-old strength that underpins our success as a species. Which is why very soon we will let that fear go.

But the fear is real. In a study of nearly 1800 CEOs and senior executives, IBM found that many leaders feel out of their depth with respect to technology. There are many reasons for this including that many executives did not grow up with technology. They may have used computers for the first time at university or even at work.

Compare that with digital natives or those who were born in the digital era, for whom using technology is as natural as throwing a ball (come to think of it, often more natural). Executives see digital natives come into a business as graduates and think they are a whole internet generation ahead of them.

But just because you feel comfortable with technology does not mean that you know anything about business strategy, or how to deal with a complex stakeholder relationship or manage a crisis.

I've often thought that the generation gap (and let's face it, this is nothing new) provides an excellent opportunity for reverse mentoring. Digital natives can take the sting out of technology by showing digital migrants how easy it is, just as migrants (most of us) can share the enormously valuable things that we've learned over a lifetime at work.

There is also a responsibility for all of us to become more digitally literate.

One reason that executives have been so slow to adopt technology is that we simply do not know enough about it, and this is something that can be easily addressed by education. Just as leaders must be able to read P&Ls and cash flows without being accountants, so too should they be able to assess the opportunities and risks of digital on the shape of business without an expectation that they are technocrats.

Having said that, given the importance of digital literacy for the future of business, should it be a prerequisite for taking a leadership role? We have to ask the question.

The key thing to remember here is that digital literacy is a skill, and like any skill it can be learned. But it's also a mindset and developing a pro-social approach is entirely in your hands.

Chapter summary

Leaders can develop a social leadership mindset by:

- educating themselves on the value of digital and social media for their industry

- evolving business models that respond to the speed of change

- skilling themselves and their people to deal with uncertainties

- developing digital and social media literacies.

CHAPTER 4

The high cost of social executive absenteeism

Are executives laggards? Let's restrict the discussion here to social media, where the data tells a conflicted tale. On the one hand, executives definitely seem behind the eight ball when it comes to using social media.

A 2012 US study of CEOs of *Fortune* 500 companies by software company Domo found that only 16 per cent were using social media. On the face of it, a doubling in their 2013 survey to 30 per cent seems significant, but this reflects the sign-up rate rather than active use. In other words, executives are signing up to platforms because they think they should but are not doing anything much once they get there—a bit like going to a business lunch and standing in the corner.

Domo founder Josh James believes these CEOs are hurting their business results and doing their shareholders a massive disservice. Although social media takes significant time and commitment, he argues, 'If you're not speaking for yourself, other people will speak for you. And you may not like what they have to say'.

A 2012 study by Stanford University's Graduate School of Business into the executive social media gap found a similar disconnect. The study 'What Do Corporate Directors and Senior Managers Know about Social Media?', which surveyed more than 180 senior executives, found no link between executive understanding of the importance of social media and action.

The study lead, Professor David F. Larcker, said the results showed that executives were well aware of the potential benefits as well as the risks of social media but were not doing a lot about it, primarily because they did not know how to make sense of social media data.

The study reached the following conclusions:

- While 90 per cent of respondents claim to understand the impact that social media can have on their organisation, only 32 per cent of their companies monitor social media.

- Just 14 per cent use metrics from social media to measure corporate performance.

- Only 24 per cent of senior managers and 8 per cent of directors get reports with social media metrics.

- Nearly 65 per cent of respondents were signed up to or used social media for personal purposes, mostly because they had a LinkedIn or Facebook account.

- Still, only 59 per cent of companies used social media to interact with customers and only 35 per cent use it for customer research.

'The Evolution of Social Business', a survey of 698 executives by Altimeter Group, also found that only around half of executives in a company were aware of or aligned with their social business strategy (that's in organisations that have one). It found that organisations where executives do not use social technologies were limited in their understanding of its power as a business tool.

Absenteeism comes at a high cost.

Writer Richard Levick, picked by *NACD Directorship* magazine as one of the '100 Most Influential People in the Boardroom', argues that leaders well aware of their responsibilities are content to let others control the online narratives that dominate public perception. He says that most directors expect their company's digital and social media strategy to be managed without their leadership but that this passive approach has allowed adversaries to leap 'a full Internet generation' ahead of the companies they target.

'Adversaries control the conversation.'

Having said that, awareness that social media is important is high and growing. For the past decade, IBM has conducted a longitudinal study of C-suites across 70 countries called the IBM Global C-Suite Study. Since 2004 CEOs have consistently identified market forces as the biggest driver of change, but for the first time in 2012 they identified technology as having the strongest influence on their organisation and strategy. The importance of managing digital disruption and social media was reinforced in the 2013 survey.

A global study of C-suite executives by MIT Sloan Management also showed 86 per cent believe social business will be important to their overall business in the next three years. Those leaders are readying themselves now by starting to develop a social business vision, a social strategy and social know-how at the leadership level and across the enterprise. Those who are not risk becoming less competitive.

The board appetite for information on social is also growing quickly, with McKinsey studies showing technology increasingly on the board agenda not as an IT issue but as a broader business issue. Big data, cloud computing and mobility present new opportunities and risks; technology is shaping business.

Some boards are directing risk committees to oversee cyber security.

But there are less dramatic-sounding risks associated with new entrants to the market that could be equally devastating. These include newcomers who cause industry disruptions through pricing or game-changing innovations.

According to the 2013 *Social Media Examiner Industry Report*, 86 per cent of marketers agree that social media is important for their business, up from 83 per cent in 2012.

These and other reports that show this trend indicate that social media is on the executive agenda but, whether because of anxiety or lack of time or both, they have yet to make the leap.

But they should. When C-suite executives become active on social media it increases brand trust. Moreover, customers want to find them there. In a 2012 BRANDfog survey 82 per cent of respondents stated that they were more likely to trust a company whose CEO and leadership team engaged on social media.

That's you.

Chapter summary

Right now leaders are lagging when it comes to using social media. Ensure that you're informed about it and know the best way to be involved.

CHAPTER 5

Double jeopardy: why you can't not be there

It's impossible not to be involved in social media. Why?

- You can be drawn in when you don't want to be.
- New media allows people to speak out.
- People in your organisation use it.
- The law says so.

Let's look at these in turn.

You can be drawn in

There are many ways, good and bad, that you can be impacted by social media even if you don't want to be.

Because the media focuses on what happens when things go wrong, so will I, not to reinforce the scaremongering but to talk through what we've learned from these crises and how they can be prevented and managed, and to demonstrate that, whether you like it or not, you're part of the socially connected world.

But a caveat. Most of the time what is going on online is business as usual. Yes there are the horror stories of the Facebook party that turned wild, or trolls tweet-bombing insults or bullies who extend their offensive behaviour into the online world. Most of the time, though, people go about their daily business, forming strategic and serendipitous connections with others who share their interests and values and for whom the name of the game is reciprocity. And because of what we've learned, when the offenders do come out, social media platforms have ways of dealing with them.

That said, let's look at what happens when things go wrong. We'll start with one of the worst things that could happen to a person—being falsely accused of being a paedophile. This happened in Britain in November 2012, and here's the backstory.

A normally reputable BBC current affairs program, *Newsnight*, aired an exposé of alleged abuse in children's homes in North Wales in the 1970s and 1980s, during which one victim, Steve Messham, claimed that one of his abusers was a Tory politician from the Thatcher era.

These allegations were publicised before *Newsnight* went to air, including on Twitter. Responding to a question from a Twitter follower as to who the politician was, one of the *Newsnight* team let out Lord McAlpine's name. It was immediately retweeted and spread like wildfire across the web.

However, the allegations were false. The Prime Minister ordered an inquiry into the matter and the Director-General of the BBC, George Entwistle, resigned the following day.

Lord McAlpine subsequently sued the BBC and threatened to sue anyone on Twitter who had shared the false accusation, data that is very easy to obtain. Had he followed through, the case would have had the largest number of defendants in British legal history. Instead, McAlpine focused on those influencers who retweeted or shared the story and whose large Twitter followings helped give the incident global legs.

Although there were many other issues raised by the case, including those of fact checking and right of reply, the real awakening was in the social media sphere. The internet is not the Wild West. The case reinforced the point that people on social media are 'publishers' responsible for their views. As to how being online impacts behaviour and how best to deal with it, these questions are still evolving.

There is, however, one simple lesson to draw from the McAlpine case, which is not to engage in malicious gossip, particularly in a public space. This is not radically different from how people are expected to behave offline. Know when to engage and when to step back; and remember, social media is not a coffee shop, it's a publication.

New media allows people to speak out

Few media-related incidents are as dramatic or damaging as this one was. But new media does allow ordinary people to comment publicly on events and to circulate their views on a scale previously restricted to the powerfully entrenched traditional media outlets.

For example, in 2012 radio talk show host Alan Jones proposed that then Prime Minister Julia Gillard's father had died of shame at her behaviour (not surprisingly, there is a wiki detailing this affair). Although Jones later apologised, many were unconvinced by the gesture. Online views around the issue quickly coalesced, and advertisers were pressured to withdraw their support from the show. Many did, and announced that decision online, predominantly on their Twitter accounts. These included Mercedes-Benz Hornsby, Woolworths, Freedom Furniture, Lexus of Parramatta, Coles, ING, Bing Lee, Mazda, 7-Eleven, Sydney Symphony Orchestra and HCF Health Insurance. This 'boycott' cost 2GB up to $80 000 per day.

Quite inadvertently, brands had become associated with the values espoused by Jones and sought to distance themselves from his actions. The broadcaster later claimed this was cyberbullying, although it did not label Jones's own comments in the same way. Those companies that did not withdraw advertising came under pressure to explain themselves. None of these businesses had woken up that morning expecting to have to justify their marketing approach to millions of people on prime-time television on the evening news, but this is the speed and impact of connected communication.

Only a year earlier advertisers pulled their support for a breakfast show after host Kyle Sandilands made misogynist comments. Once again, online communities used new media to express their outrage at what many believed was an abuse of media power.

People in your organisation use it

This sort of reputational entanglement can also work in reverse. People all around the world as well as within your organisation use social media. Regardless of whether that's professional or personal, you need to know how to handle it.

Sometimes this happens at the most senior levels. American congressman Anthony Weiner was forced to resign in 2011 after sending sexually explicit material via Twitter to a 21-year-old female college student. When he tried to return to politics in 2013 as a mayoral candidate for New York City he was alleged to have continued his sexting behaviour under the alias 'Carlos Danger'.

In Australia the A-League soccer team Melbourne Victory, the Melbourne Rebels rugby union team and the AFL club Melbourne Demons all dumped a major sponsor, Energy Watch, after its CEO, Ben Pollis, posted a string of racist, sexist and bigoted messages on his personal but publicly visible

Facebook page. Pollis's targets ranged from Aborigines and Asians to various religious groups, women and Prime Minister Julia Gillard. Although he claimed these were private jokes, they were of course public and as the owner of the Facebook page Pollis was responsible for the comments. The boards of the various sports clubs met immediately and very quickly terminated their sponsorships with the business, as did other businesses such as Momentum Energy and TruEnergy who were using the energy broker.

These were not trivial decisions. For the Demons alone, the deal was worth around $6 million over three years. The energy companies also lost money as a result of these resolutions, and of course the CEO was forced to resign, the company went into receivership and employees lost their entitlements.

The personal and professional are intertwined when views are expressed in public forums. A man in Canada lost his job when he used Twitter to try to score marijuana. He tweeted: 'Any dealers in Vaughan wanna make a 20sac chop? Come to Keele/Langstaff Mr. Lube, need a spliff'. Police who saw the tweet shared it with the added comment, 'Awesome! Can we come too?' The tweet quickly received 3710 retweets and 2456 'favourites'. Because there was no crime, no charges were laid but police did inform his employer, who subsequently fired him.

White House staffer Jofi Joseph also lost his job when it was revealed he was running an anonymous Twitter account, @natsecwonk, that criticised top officials in the foreign policy and national security communities.

The stories go on, although hopefully we are learning. But the common lesson of all of them is simple: social media is a publishing platform; when you use it, you are a publisher and you're responsible for what you say. And whether you like it or not, because so many people use it, social media affects you in some way.

Which brings us to the law.

The law says so

Although there is increasing awareness about social media, and companies realise that they need to be where their customers are, there is still a view that social media is about the sales, communication or marketing space. But this approach fails to recognise that the impacts of a channel that is ubiquitous are themselves ubiquitous, and that social media can directly and very quickly impact the market. Managing it, therefore, has to be wholly integrated into corporate strategy, governance and risk. Fortunately, the market is responding to this need and new technologies are becoming available.

The Brandle Presence Manager is one that I am aware of that provides a centralised system for businesses to discover what digital and social assets are out there, create an inventory and monitor where it is being said across all the business social media platforms. This is social media governance and compliance at the enterprise level.

Here's an example.

In 2013 US stocks plunged temporarily when an announcement about a bomb at the White House was made via the Associated Press Twitter account, which had been hacked. Action by Twitter (which suspended the account) and AP ensured the account was quickly taken offline. But the tweet was shared over 3000 times in the few minutes that it remained up. AP immediately confirmed the news was not true, but the Dow Jones nevertheless plunged 120 points within a couple of minutes and reached 143 points down before it recovered. Subsequent reports suggest over $20 billion worth of stock changed hands during the brief trading hiccup.

Also last year in the US, tweets sent from a hoax Twitter account disguised as a well-known equity research group caused a sell-off in a Silicon Valley company. This potentially illegal act of financial manipulation was subsequently investigated by the US regulator.

In August 2012 an Italian journalist set up a fake Twitter account for a member of Russia's government and tweeted that the President of Syria had been killed, causing brief fluctuations in the oil markets.

And in January 2013 in Australia the share price of listed company Whitehaven Coal dropped 6 per cent after a fake press release lit up the online networks. The release, claimed to be from the ANZ Bank, asserted that a recent loan to Whitehaven had been withdrawn, which would have had a significant impact on its Maules Creek project. Both Whitehaven and the ANZ later confirmed the hoax, but not before $314 million was wiped off the share price and trading in the company was brought to a halt. The year before, trading in Macmahon Holdings was halted when hoax emails prompted takeover speculation, and retailer David Jones was the subject of a similar false takeover bid.

While market rumours are nothing new, social media means information (true or false) can reach people—shareholders, the media, regulators—faster than a company can respond. The potentially damaging impact of social media is not, however, limited to hoaxes.

Last year, for example, Netflix announced it had exceeded a billion hours to its 250000 Facebook subscribers, which the Securities and Exchange Commission (the US equivalent of ASIC) interpreted as a violation of Regulation Fair Disclosure. Netflix argued the announcement was very public, since its following included shareholders, bloggers and journalists.

Although there were other factors in the case (the information had already been widely shared and was not relevant to the share price), the event triggered hot debate on what legitimate conversation looks like in the social era. In April the SEC announced that social media could be used to communicate company information provided investors were told first. This decision bridges existing and emerging practice, acknowledging that social media is a legitimate and ongoing channel without letting companies off the hook with respect to existing obligations.

In the US various regulatory bodies have published guidelines on the use of social media. The UK has limited new regulatory guidance on social media with respect to monitoring, communication, promotion and market abuse.

In Australia, working closely with ASIC, the Australian Stock Exchange updated its guidance on disclosure in 2013, advising companies to monitor online for sensitive information to ensure that the market trades fully informed. Further, company secretaries must consider its impacts with respect to risk. The ASX was clear that it did not expect companies to monitor every single comment but only for market-sensitive information, material transactions and market speculation. The Australian Competition and Consumer Commission (ACCC) has said all businesses should monitor platforms and have 24 hours (or longer for small businesses) to act on misleading information. Businesses are responsible for comments made by others on their sites.

Irrespective of the country you live in and the laws that apply in that jurisdiction, you need to be thinking about monitoring social media and managing its impact on recruitment, training, liability, confidentiality, privacy, security, advertising, IP, consumers and third parties, to name but a few.

Here again, monitoring tools give you a complete picture of your social footprint and a way to protect your IP. Brandle, for example, allows you to discover authorised and unauthorised uses of corporate IP and monitor your designated inventory for regulatory compliance to ensure proper disclosures are present.

In Australia I have recently been talking to Note8; a social tool that helps companies manage ASX listing requirements. There are sure to be more of these, which will make governance easier.

Why do you have to pay attention to social media? It impacts every area of life and with ever more people expected to go online and predictions that the social media audience will reach 2.55 billion by 2017, these impacts are set to increase.

Chapter summary

Whether you like it or not, you are involved in social media. Ensure that you:

- have a social media crisis strategy in place
- have the right governance—put policies in place to manage its use and ensure appropriate controls at the board or executive level
- know what the law says in your country.

CHAPTER 6

Professional development at the digital frontier

Is there no end to the utility and potential of connected communication? For a self-declared tech (and all-round) optimist, I think not. Connected networks allow unprecedented collaboration, which has created a giant global brain that is powering us forward, and it's open to anyone who can access the internet.

Tapping into this global brain, for example when we type a question into Google, is so routine that we don't stop to think about the enormous complexity of the algorithms that bring us answers or the billions of humans who participate in creating and linking web pages to provide that information.

Of course, the principle of pooling resources, including intellectual ones, to improve outcomes for the tribe is as old as human history. But in the past resources were tightly held and access was often associated with privilege. The internet has opened things up.

In the past the printing press monks painstakingly transcribed books by hand, and few people knew how to read anyway. But once information started flowing freely, people were incentivised to learn to read and education flourished, as did the circulation of new ideas.

Now anyone online can learn practically anything for free, including from prestigious universities around the world. This makes 'access' the new gold currency, and groups like Internet.org and Google aim to bridge the digital divide and bring the internet to the two-thirds of the world not yet adequately connected.

Of course there's always a downside and these technologies can be used for ill, as with every such innovation that came before them. We've seen examples of the crowd turning on others or sharing inaccurate information, and in the digital world, as in real life, there are laws for dealing with these issues.

Professor Thomas W. Malone, founder of the MIT Center for Collective Intelligence, dubs the shadow side of the crowd 'collective stupidity'. His research centre is working to understand the conditions that lead in one direction rather than the other so we can consciously harness collective intelligence for good.

So having added that caveat, let's look at some of the amazing gifts of connected communication and, in particular, their role in professional development. These include:

- open learning
- crowdsourcing
- crowdfunding
- gaming
- customer service

- disaster management
- open government.

Open learning

Education changes everything. With education we live longer, are healthier and less prone to violence, and make better decisions. It's not a panacea—life is complex—but it's one of the most powerful tools we have for developing collective wellbeing.

The National Bureau of Economic Research tells us: 'An additional four years of education lowers five-year mortality by 1.8 percentage points; it also reduces the risk of heart disease by 2.16 percentage points, and the risk of diabetes by 1.3 percentage points'.

A major contributor to education is the online open learning movement, through which access to high-quality courses from prestigious universities is helping people to extend their skill base.

There's enormous potential in this approach to break down geographic, economic, racial and gender barriers. And there's evidence this is happening through initiatives such as the Khan Academy, which offers free science and maths tuition in places like rural India. But there's also evidence that already multi-degreed people are using it to further hone their skills or develop new ones and even reposition themselves within their careers.

Open learning is contributing enormously to the development of the knowledge economy or knowledge society. For those of us wishing to remain relevant and employable into the increasingly global interconnected and competitive future, it's gold.

Let's have a look at some of what is on offer.

MOOCs

A Massive Open Online Course (MOOC), accessed via the web, provides a combination of traditional and interactive course materials such as videos, readings and problem sets.

There are many free online education platforms that we'll look at shortly. But first, a story about the first 100 000-student classroom.

The 100 000-student classroom

In 2011 Stanford professor Sebastian Thrun and Peter Norvig, director of research at Google, decided to open up their Introduction to Artificial Intelligence course to the world.

In a sense, all roads had been leading to this Rome, with enthusiasts of open learning at Stanford University like Daphne Koller and Andrew Ng having championed its potential in the previous years. Having made the announcement that the beginners AI course would be available free to anyone who wanted to access it, the sign-up started. Within days, more than 100 000 people had registered.

The bell rang and eager students from 130 countries around the world and many different time zones tuned in to hear the streamed lectures and participate in the Q and A sessions.

Recalling the class later, Norwig wrote: 'What kept me most engaged throughout the course was the attitude of the public students, conveyed primarily through emails and posts on the Q&A Forum. They were unabashedly, genuinely, deeply appreciative. Many said the course was a gift they could scarcely believe had come their way. As the course came to a close, several students admitted to shedding tears. One posted a heartfelt poem' (http://wp.sigmod.org/?p=165).

Now, artificial intelligence is a rarified subject, and yet 100 000 people signed up. Imagine the potential in other areas.

Although participants did not receive a Stanford-endorsed certificate, they learned the same information as those who were formally enrolled in the course. This potential for restructuring paid education business models is being closely examined. Few can afford an education at Ivy League universities, yet everywhere around the world people are willing to invest in their education, which many see as a ticket out of poverty.

If 10 students pay $50 000 a year but hundreds of thousands of students are willing to commit themselves there may be a way to monetise these in the future. Of course, just how to certify that the person who is doing the course is who they say they are and finding ways to prevent cheating will be challenging. But technology is getting smarter at recognising patterns in the way we think and write, so this may soon be possible.

Although the course was dominated by participants from (in descending order) the USA, India and Russia, it attracted people from every continent. Their ages and occupations varied, but most were professionals seeking to sharpen their skills. Check it out at db-class.org.

Soon other prestigious universities, such as MIT, followed suit and there are now numerous free online education platforms around the world.

Some of the world's best-known free online education platforms

- *Coursera*—a free online platform that features over 200 courses from 33 universities like Stanford

- *Udacity*—offers accessible, affordable, interactive online courses with a focus on careers in technology. Courses are developed with leaders in the tech industry to bridge the gap between academia and the needs of the 21st-century workforce. Units range from Introduction to Computer Science to Data Wrangling with MongoDB.

(continued)

Some of the world's best-known free online education platforms (cont'd)

- *Iversity*—courses are delivered by professors and are conducted mainly in English or German, but also in Russian and Italian. Courses include but are not limited to DNA, Dark Matter, Medicine, Storytelling, Internet Privacy, Web Engineering, Architecture, Math, Statistics, Algorithms, Finance, Political Philosophy, Social Entrepreneurship, Business, Marketing and Agricultural Science.

- *edX*—MIT, Harvard and 29 other schools offer university-level courses in a wide range of disciplines to a worldwide audience at no charge. EdX has nearly 1.6 million users.

Other providers include Canvas Network, Open Learning, Academic Earth, Future Learn, Peer to Peer University, Saylor, org, Udemy, MOOEC, World Education Portals and First Business MOOC.

One of my favourite stories, though, brings us back to Khan Academy. I love its serendipitous roots and the focus on making maths and science, such critical skills in a technology-driven age, accessible to all.

Khan Academy

Salmat Khan used to tutor his cousins in maths and science. One day he couldn't make it so decided to video the tutorial instead. What he learned, he would later joke, is that they preferred him on video than in person. Not only did they learn what they needed to learn but they were able to share that video with friends who also needed the additional output. And in one of the happiest accidents of modern times, Khan Academy was born.

Khan Academy is a non-profit educational website that aims to offer a free world-class education for anyone anywhere. Like the MOOC it includes content, interactive challenges, assessments and videos, but the focus is on science and maths.

What I love about Khan Academy is the principle-based approach. Learning is self-paced and students are able to repeat a class as often as it takes them to learn the principles. It's also possible to generate different exercises so you can approach the topic from a number of angles.

Why is this so important? We live in a world where, rightly or wrongly, intelligence is equated with fast learning. And our education systems are set up to privilege those who learn fast. Students who learn slowly or struggle with a certain concept can be disadvantaged when a teacher needs to move on. The problem with subjects like maths is that one principle builds on another. You're not going to understand calculus if you failed to understand multiples. There's no blame around this; teachers are under huge pressure to move through curriculum material at a pace that suits the majority of the students. But being able to access these materials anytime, and progress at your own pace, without anyone thinking you're dumb, raises the bar.

Some poor rural states in India that cannot afford teachers and textbooks have partnered with Khan Academy so the educational material matches the school syllabus. (These can be found on an affiliated website, teachersofindia.org.) Attendance rates soared at schools once the video material became available.

But affluent and poor alike are using Khan Academy in blended learning arrangements or for professional development.

As a parent, I find that my maths knowledge is seriously outdated. If my boys ask me a question I will often sit down with them to watch a Khan video so we can learn together. I can then reinforce the learning by asking them questions or working through problems together with them.

Professional development

Although MOOCs and learning academies like Khan were established to level the playing field, the reality is they have become one of the most important vocational training tools.

Research conducted by the University of Pennsylvania's Graduate School of Education and published in the journal *Nature* shows that some 80 per cent of MOOC users around the world already have an advanced degree, with up to 80 per cent of students coming from the richest 6 per cent of the population.

This means the skilled are becoming more skilled.

It's still early days for online learning and, as with all innovations, we are likely to learn by getting things wrong as well as getting things right and making continual iterations. However, the experiment to date combined with the Penn research reinforces the conclusion that access to computers and the internet is critical for countries to remain competitive. All sorts of projects to increase connectivity are underway.

Raspberry Pi is a credit card–sized computer that costs between $25 and $35, and plugs into your TV; a keyboard can boot into a programming environment. Project Loon involves a network of balloons travelling on the edge of space connecting wirelessly to the internet via a handful of ground stations, and passing signals to one another in a kind of daisy chain. The aim is to help fill coverage gaps, provide internet access to rural and remote areas, and bring people back online after natural disasters. But that's another story, for another day.

MOOCs are accepted by many employers as providing legitimate training. Employees are posting the accreditations they receive at these course on their LinkedIn profiles or showing certificates at their job interview, and employers generally regard them highly.

Open culture

Open culture brings together free high-quality cultural and educational content including:

- business courses
- online and certificate courses—almost 1000 free and 800 MOOC or certificate courses curated, from astronomy and biology through economics, history and maths all the way to religion
- movies—over 600 free movies, from early silent films to documentaries, animations and film noir and all the way to Oscar winners
- audio books—fiction, poetry, non-fiction, sci-fi and the classics
- ebooks
- textbooks
- language lessons—including Arabic, Chinese, English, German, Russian, Spanish … and much more; and as this is curation it will lead you to sites like duolingo
- kids' education.

Code: a future language in the future of business?

If a language is a set of symbols around which there is a shared understanding, then there's no doubt that code is a new global language.

This doesn't mean every professional needs to know how to code, any more than they had to know how to build a personal computer before being able to use one or a desk before having a place to work. But in a world in which people and products are increasingly interconnected through code, understanding the principles of codification needs to become part of our mindset. And given the pace of change driven by technology and given that technology makes more technology possible, to use Alvin Toffler's phrase, it could be as important in the future to accessing knowledge about the world as knowing how to read and write once was.

Like social media, some people 'in the know' have mystified the code and have created a subculture that makes it seem frightening and inaccessible to the ordinary person. But coding is a skill. It requires analytical and creative thinking and if you break it down to that level it is familiar and doable.

There are also those who understand the benefits of knowing how to code and are graciously sharing their knowledge with the masses. If you are interested, the web is full of resources that allow you to learn to code in any language, and for free.

Some web resources offering online code instruction

- At Codecademy, you can take lessons on writing simple commands in JavaScript, HTML and CSS, Python and Ruby.

- Code School offers online courses in a wide range of programming languages, design and web tools.

- Girl Develop It is an international nonprofit that provides mentorship and instruction to girls. Girls Who Code is geared towards 13- to 17-year-olds and Black Girls Code aims to help address the 'dearth of African-American women in science, technology, engineering and math professions'.

- Stanford University's Udacity provide college courses such as Introduction to Computer Science. (See our post on free online courses for more ideas.)

- Code Racer is a multiplayer live coding game in which you can learn to build a website using HTML and CSS. The parent site, Treehouse, provides online video courses and exercises to help you learn technology skills. Rails for Zombies is similar.

- Other programs, such as Computer Clubhouse and CoderDojo, work with professional or volunteer-led mentors.

- Microsoft has a beginner coding development centre and is working with organisations like Code.org in the US to bring computer science into schools, including through the annual hour of code event.

And if all this seems overwhelming and you don't know where to start, educators all over the internet are making suggestions about how to go about it. If you Google 'Medium' (a global, open publishing platform) you will find several good curations specifically built around coding. But don't limit yourself by where you look.

I loved an approach by David Sinsky that I have truncated below. (Who is he? Just a person, like you or me, who taught himself to code and then kindly shared what he had learned on Medium. I like this thinking process.)

1   Learn the key programming terms
    (http://viniciusvacanti.com/2010/11/01/6-things-you-need-to-learn-to-build-your-own-prototype/).

2   Get a grasp using Learn Python the hard way
    (http://learnpythonthehardway.org/book/) or Google's Python class (https://developers.google.com/edu/python/introduction?csw=1).

3   Learn Django
    (https://docs.djangoproject.com/en/1.4/intro/tutorial01/).

4   Delete your code.

5   Work through the tutorial again.

6   Improve your Python
    (https://www.udacity.com/course/viewer#!/c-cs101/l-48299949/m-48698544).

7   Do an introduction to computer science
    (http://ocw.mit.edu/courses/electrical-engineering-and-computer-science/6-00sc-introduction-to-computer-science-and-programming-spring-2011/).

8   Practise.

9   Build a prototype.

This sequence will look very familiar to anyone involved in training, and not that different from how to use Microsoft Word or read financial reports.

Crowdsourcing: business opportunity or business threat?

Crowdsourcing is another trend made possible by globally connected platforms. Crowdsourcing is the digital equivalent of 'many hands make light work'. It allows you to access the collective brain for answers to problems or to contribute to tasks. It can be paid—such as sourcing a designer on a freelancing site—or unpaid. The principle is the same.

This is how crowdsourcing is being used and, depending on who you are and how you see it, it can be an opportunity or a threat.

Paid crowdsourcing

There are now plenty of online platforms that connect employers and freelancers. You can work with a freelancer on a discrete project (designing a logo, say) or in an ongoing capacity by outsourcing website management to a platform such as Tweak. These are the equivalent of the specialist guns for hire that organisations used extensively in the past—without needing to account for a position on payroll. Here are some examples:

- Freelancer and eLance are online job marketplaces that bring together employers and freelancers. If you need short- or long-term help on a project you post the job and freelancers submit bids. One benefit is immediacy. Employers can also avoid costs associated with advertising, office space, insurance and so forth.

- 99 Designs is a marketplace for graphic design. Submit a brief and hundreds of freelancers join in a competition to present the design that you ultimately purchase.

- Elto helps you to implement multiple improvements to your website. They break down the list you submit into tweaks and charge you a small amount for each. This has been a godsend for many people who are not technologically savvy but who need small improvements to their sites. They may not have a full-time webmaster and many web developers will not take on this sort of work because it's too small.

- Similarly, Fiverr helps you to find experts to take on (for as little as $5) those small, unusual tasks that need doing and for which you definitely do not need a full-time role—recording a voiceover, designing a corporate Christmas card or giving you five ideas for your blog.

People use crowdsourcing because the strong competition can result in much lower prices for products of equal quality. From a global perspective it can be a win–win situation. You might pay $500 for a logo that would cost thousands if you commissioned it locally, at the same time paying someone in a developing country a hundred times the standard monthly wage. There can be costs to the local market (companies like Sidekicker aim to overcome these). Some professionals refuse to work on crowdsourced sites because the effort put in to win competitions is not always rewarded. However, they are great for startup companies that are not well resourced but still need the same collateral as more established businesses.

As a professional this opens up lots of possibilities:

- If you're prepared to work virtually you can source specialist expertise from anywhere around the world, rather than just locally.

- You can also sell your skills globally by working full time as a freelancer or supplementing traditional work. I know of several people who left the traditional workplace and are earning as much or even more money working this way.

Crowdsourcing platforms

There are hundreds of crowdsourcing platforms across all industries that cover everything from the general to the highly specific. Here are just a few:

- BigCarrot (problem solving)
- CastingWords (transcription)
- CGILance.com (programmers)
- Crowdsifter (Dolores Labs) (content moderation)
- CrowdSpring (graphic design)
- GetACoder.com (programming)
- Jobtonic.com (job referral)
- Kluster (customer surveying)
- LeadVine (sales leads)
- LivePerson (expert help)
- NamingForce (product naming)
- oDesk (project marketplace).

Unpaid crowdsourcing

The time and effort that unpaid citizens are putting into hobbies they love that are being coordinated by organisations with a purpose is contributing significantly to the global brain and what is commonly referred to as the 'knowledge economy'. Businesses are also using the crowd to source customer research and feedback, or even to come up with names and designs for new products.

Crowdsourcing for business

- Madrid crowdsourced the logo for its 2020 Olympics bid in a country-wide design contest. The London Olympics' 2012 logo cost £400 000; Madrid's cost just €6000.

- Chip company Frito-Lay asked consumers to help come up with a new flavour in the 'Do Us a Flavor' campaign, awarding $1 million to the winning entrant.

- Google relies on the collective intelligence of billions of webpage links. In 2012 it launched the Consumer Insights tool, which helps businesses gather opinions from the crowd for 10 cents a pop.

- Budweiser crowdsourced its new beer, Black Crown, through Project 12, which asked 12 brewers to come up with a new product. Consumers were then asked to pick the one they liked best. A whopping 25 000 consumers voted, and the majority chose the Black Crown beer.

Citizen science

The old saying that 'information is power' meant just that in the past. Organisations believed their data provided strategic advantage and protected it tightly. The internet has led to a radical shift in thinking on this, because it has shown that when you make data openly available, people can use it in constructive ways that benefit not only you but the world more broadly. *Open data* is the idea that certain data should be available for people to use however they like without copyright or patent restrictions, and there are now huge open data movements (see, for example, data.gov and data.gov.uk).

Here are a few of the amazing things that people have been able to contribute by using other people's data.

Finding new planets

Many armchair astronomers spend countless hours of their personal time staring up at the sky, simply because they love it. And while in the past they did this purely for personal satisfaction they can now make a real contribution to science through their hobby.

For example, Yale University established Planet Hunters (planethunters.org), which brings together the expertise of professional and citizen astronomers, and which in October 2012 led to the discovery of a planet that is orbiting a double-star, which in turn is orbited by a second, distant pair of stars.

Involving citizens in science does not compromise scientific rigour. Once discoveries are made they are brought in-house to be verified, as in this case, where the Yale-led team confirmed the discovery.

Mapping the galaxy

Planet Hunters was launched after the huge success of Galaxy Zoo.

The first citizen science project, Galaxy Zoo sourced amateur astronomers to help classify data collected by a robotic telescope from over a million galaxies. When this science portal was launched in 2007 so many people tried to sign up to help that the site went down.

In its second phase, Galaxy Zoo 283000 citizen scientists helped catalogue 300000 galaxies. To date, 54 scientific papers have been published based on Zooniverse's crowdsourced data. In total, citizen scientists made 16 million morphological classifications.

Citizen journalism

Paul Lewis is a multi-awarded journalist from *The Guardian* newspaper in the United Kingdom. He is famous for using social media to investigate deaths that have been wrongly attributed. In 2009 he became interested in the death of Ian Tomlinson during the G20 protests. Reports claimed Tomlinson died from a heart attack, but Lewis was suspicious. After he wrote about it in his newspaper and reached out through social media, more than 20 witnesses came forward in just six days.

As is the nature of global social media networks, this information found its way around the world, and it wasn't long before a New York businessman brought it to the attention of his investment fund manager colleague, who had been in London on business at the time. As it turned out, by chance he had recorded the event on his digital camera. The material collected showed Tomlinson being assaulted by police, who later issued an apology to Tomlinson's family and publicly admitted that his death was not the result of natural causes.

Crowdfunding

Crowdfunding is a way of funding projects through small contributions from many people. It's being used by business and individuals and is a potentially disruptive force. This is why.

Kiva

You may not have heard of the online microfinancing site Kiva. If you click on the Home page you'll see photos of people in developing countries around the world looking for loans to set up a business. You give $25, which is returned to you over time. Let's face it, even if the borrower defaulted, most of us would be happy to contribute $25—we probably spend as much a week buying coffee. But as an active Kiva supporter I receive ongoing repayments. I love the idea of Kiva because it's more than a charitable donation. It's that whole sustainable ethos of teaching someone to fish so you can feed them for life.

According to its website Kiva was founded in 2005 and can boast of:

- 1 046 375 lenders
- who have given $525 399 650 in loans

- with a 98.96 per cent repayment rate
- working with 240 Field Partners and 450 volunteers in 73 different countries around the world.

But the really interesting part of this story is that microfinance was once the exclusive domain of banks. Platforms like Kiva are carving out a niche that was inaccessible only a decade or so ago. Established players should not take their territory for granted.

Kickstarter

Kickstarter is a crowdfunding platform for, broadly speaking, creativity. So far $220 million has been pledged and 61 000 projects launched.

It's often difficult to fund the arts, particularly in countries that do not have active arts philanthropists. Even when governments offer grants there can be only a few winners. By allowing individuals to contribute small amounts to projects they genuinely believe in, far more artists have a chance of getting their work off the ground.

Singer Amanda Palmer broke records last year by raising well over a million dollars via crowdfunding to pay for the recording of her new album. At the time, it was the biggest sum raised by any musician through a Kickstarter campaign.

There are now crowdfunding sites for every kind of project. There are also signs that crowdfunding could be used in the future for investment. This will be a big issue for lawmakers and regulators.

Governments are also using crowdsourcing, in particular for community projects. The New York City Council created an official page on Kickstarter that is a hub for community projects in low-income areas. In the English Midlands, Mansfield District Council successfully used Spacehive to raise over £36 000 to install free WiFi in the town. Bristol

City Council crowdfunded grants for local charities and social enterprises that work with disadvantaged youth.

All this has led to all sorts of discussions, including whether there should be tax breaks for those who contribute to community projects.

Crowdfunding sites

Here is a sampling of interesting crowdfunding sites:

- Indiegogo — for independent personal projects
- Rockethub — prepares a project for launch working with top-notch brands, companies and marketers to help them raise public interest in projects
- Gofundme — specialises in raising money online for a cause or personal campaign
- Razoo — has raised $97 million for thousands of fundraising causes in four major categories: nonprofits, individuals, corporations and foundations.
- Crowdrise — raises money for real-world issues such as animal welfare, disease prevention and education, and charity.
- Pledgemusic — aims to bring new talent into the music industry
- Sellaband — coordinates recording sessions (has provided $4 million of funding for musicians)
- Appbackr — finds backers for apps that are under development or on sale
- Crowdfunder — allows US startup and small businesses to raise funds by selling equity, debt and revenue-based securities, while attracting Angel Investors and Venture Capital
- Spacehive
- Pozible (Aus).

Typically people who choose to crowdfund projects receive a reward, such as early access to a software program, and all the platforms take a percentage of what is raised in fees. However, the increased use of crowdfunding is causing some regulators to rethink their approach.

In the US the Securities and Exchange Commission has tabled rules that would help guide a new investment strategy known as equity crowdfunding. Regular investors would be able to invest in startups via crowdfunding in exchange for company equity, previously available only to accredited investors. The new rules would allow startups to raise up to $1 million from donors online over a 12-month period.

Gaming

Do you think gaming is a waste of time and energy? Many people do. But increasingly we're learning that a gaming mindset can provide a competitive advantage.

Famous among game thinkers is Dr Jane McGonigal, a game developer who believes that gaming can make us emotionally healthier and more productive. Scientific trials of her game SuperBetter indicated that it helped players tackle real-life health challenges such as depression, anxiety, chronic pain and traumatic brain injury.

A competitive advantage

Companies like Deloitte use gamification techniques as part of executive development. At NTT Data the use of gamification to develop leaders is also showing business results. Using the Ignite Leadership game, NTT Data leaders learn key leadership skills such as negotiation, communication, time management, change management and problem solving while collaborating with each other and receiving immediate feedback from their peers.

But the value of gaming is only just starting to be understood. Combined with crowdsourcing, it's proving to be a powerful source of answers to some of life's most difficult questions.

Games can solve wicked science problems

Recently a couple of scientists joined forces to develop a game to solve a tricky biochemical problem — protein folding. Conquering it could support the development of drugs for some of today's incurable diseases.

It's essential to know the stable shape of a protein if you want to create a drug that can interact with it, say in disease. But proteins can fold in multiple and complex ways. So complex that even powerful computers like the Rosetta program developed by Professor David Barker have achieved very limited results.

Barker and a colleague from the University of Washington's Center for Game Science, Professor David Salesin, believed that bringing people with excellent spatial reasoning and problem-solving skills together with the computer program would achieve a better result. By appealing to gamers they believed they could tap into that mindset. So they created a protein folding game called Foldit and released it to the world.

Foldit presents users with a simulated structure of a protein. The player 'folds' the protein (rearranging its shape) until it achieves a unique and stable structure. Gamers using Foldit recently helped unlock the structure of an AIDS-related enzyme that the scientific community had been puzzling over for a decade. Two papers have been published in the prestigious science journal *Nature* drawing on Foldit discoveries. The creators have now brought together scientists to try to find a cure for sepsis, or blood poisoning. Sepsis causes the body to become inflamed after an infection. There are more than 100 million cases of the disease each year and it can be fatal. Crowdsourcing could generate more solutions in a more efficient way.

Customer service and care

A globally connected world means we are always open for business. Certainly customers see it this way. They want to be able to reach a business when and how they want, and they expect support to be available 24/7.

That may seem overwhelming but if you think about it, why should someone who spends $50 on a shirt one night not be able to expect the same level of support for spending the same amount of money in the morning? Social media customer service should be a key component of any business strategy.

Although working out how to deliver social media customer service may require rethinking on the part of businesses, social media can be fast and effective for resolving complaints. The very public airing companies receive when things go wrong can seem frightening, but the upside is that the resolution is equally visible, leaving a good taste in the mouth for thousands.

With respect to customer care, compared with traditional CRM, *Business Insider* suggests that social customer management could double the percentage of sales leads that result in actual sales. But businesses are not yet delivering well in this space. A 2011 study by social media analytics company evolve24 found that approximately 70 per cent of customer service complaints made on Twitter go unanswered.

Social media strategist and author Jay Baer believes the provision of customer service via social media channels has become 'nearly axiomatic', especially in B2C industries, and that there are no awards for just turning up. Customers have high expectations. Research from The Social Habit shows that when customers look for support in social media, 32 per cent of them expect a response within 30 minutes and 42 per cent within 60 minutes. If brands are not resourced to respond to this need—which brings us back to immediacy—it can create what Baer calls a 'disillusionment gap'. Leading companies have been doing this successfully since 2005. Dell, for example, is into its third generation of social customer support. This is far from 'new'. As Baer says, there are no prizes for showing up here.

Research from the Avaya Asia Pacific Customer Experience Index suggests that social media is the fastest-growing customer service channel, along with mobile applications. The results showed that:

- 40 per cent of consumers using social sites value access to customer service (via The Connection)

- 70 per cent of airlines surveyed use social media to promote their brand and offer reservations, customer relationship management and check-in via social media platforms (B2C.com)

- 80 per cent of consumers heard back from brands they contacted through social media within 12 hours (eDigitalResearch)

- 59 per cent of organisations take more than one working day to respond to email complaints. The average response time on Twitter was 5.1 hours, with 10 per cent of companies answering within one hour (Simply Measured).

Crisis management

Social media has long been used for crisis management, as we will see when we look at platforms in detail. There are hundreds of case studies about its effectiveness, but now organisations are getting more sophisticated and using it as a two-way channel for disaster recovery.

In the US, for example, the Federal Emergency Management Agency (FEMA) integrated a 'Disaster Reporter' into its app that allows users to make submissions that can be hosted on the FEMA website map for public viewing. People who are impacted by a crisis almost immediately take to the airwaves with photos or comments, and this allows that information to be centralised and shared. Pictures have to be geo-tagged and the process is moderated to ensure they're not altered and don't include information that puts people at risk.

Open government

Increasingly governments are allowing people to freely access their data though portals like data.org and data.org.uk. But some politicians have gone further and are using technology to encourage real involvement in the creation of legislation.

One example, started by US Congressman Darrell Issa, is the Madison Project, an online crowdsourcing legislative platform that allows anyone to make suggestions about the drafting of legislation via an open source editing tool supporting commenting, sharing and collaboration. There may be unusual suggestions, but the process is aggressively transparent and the identity of every group or person who makes a suggestion is made public.

Think about the implications of this approach with respect to participation but also, potentially, some of the expensive and laborious red tape that is the bane of businesses worldwide. There are many people using technology solutions to help people participate in government.

Issa has since launched a foundation to expand the ability of citizens to suggest changes to all legislation, and to fund more experiments in digital participation. He is, of course, crowdsourcing developers to parse legislative text into a readable format.

Case Study

Using social media for emergency management — Department of Justice (Victoria) FireReady

Channels

- Real-time weather information using temperature-activated search ads

- YouTube

- FireReady app

Victoria, one of Australia's most densely populated states, is also one of the most fire-prone areas in the world. After the Black Saturday bushfires in 2009 during which 173 people were killed, the Department of Justice increased its focus on educating residents about the threat of bushfire. Despite previous campaigns, a survey revealed that 75 per cent of Victorians would monitor the severity of the bushfire situation before taking action. They used innovative new technologies to reach out to those who might be affected.

Temperature-activated search ads

In partnership with Google, the department used temperature-activated search ads to deliver real-time weather information. The department obtained hourly temperature data from the Bureau of Meteorology and served search ads based on the corresponding risk levels. By setting up ad parameters, the campaign was able to deliver tailored messages across multiple screens warning Victorians of the danger of fire as soon as the temperature exceeded 30 degrees Celsius. One-third of all searches came from mobiles.

Multi-platform

Multiple platforms were used to reach different demographic groups, including True View on YouTube to engage 18- to 34-year-olds.

(continued)

Case Study *(cont'd)*

Multi-language

Two separate campaigns were run across Google's Display Network to target those in rural Victoria and non-English speaking residents in Mandarin, Cantonese, Arabic and Korean languages.

FireReady app

The FireReady app was developed to meet the increasing preference for mobile service delivery and to provide simple, reliable and timely emergency information and warnings.

The app is a centralised information source that provides warnings and information from all incidents attended by fire agencies.

The new app allows people to watch zones and provide real-time warnings and information on Total Fire Bans and Fire Danger Ratings, can send 2.6 million notifications per minute and uses a Google Maps interface.

Results

- 288 000 clicks on weather active search ads including 33 per cent by mobile

- reduced Cost Per Click (CPC) by 10 per cent

- increased Click Through Rate (CT) from 8.56 per cent to 12 per cent

- more than 550 000 downloads of the app, which has sent out more than 127 million fire ratings, incidents and warnings since it was launched in late December 2013.

Chapter summary

There is no end to the utility and potential of connected communication. The networked global brain provides unprecedented access to education and new ways of learning, funding and being citizens that, used well, will power us forward.

Part II

HOW DO I USE IT?

Professionals need to secure the digital assets that will enable them to establish and grow online influence. And with hundreds of social media platforms to choose from, time-pressured executives must choose the right platforms for their profession or business to ensure their social investment is strategic.

Read the following chapters and learn how to:

- snap up your valuable digital and social media assets

- measure your online influence

- tap into the power of the global brain through Twitter

- successfully use LinkedIn for networking

- amplify your professional expertise through SlideShare

- ensure you are found and known online using Google Plus

- use Facebook to connect with family and friends

- curate, automate and implement a social strategy that will make you visible, influential and successful in an interconnected world.

CHAPTER 7

Why you must own your digital and social media assets

As in real life, so too in digital, you need to secure your assets. You are strongly advised to claim your online real estate, including your:

- domain name (the website address or URL)
- Twitter handle
- account name in LinkedIn, SlideShare, Google Plus and Facebook.

Even if you don't want to go social now, securing your digital assets is a defensive strategy. From a company point of view it's non-negotiable. Imagine an online crisis occurs and you are forced to go online to defend your reputation, only to discover someone else owns your brand names online, possibly the hijacker who caused the problem in the first place.

There are three kinds of reasons you should own your name, business name and close variations on it:

- *defensive*—to prevent parody, spoofs, impersonation and digital hijacking

- *online reputation management*—to manage online crisis and build reputation
- *forward-looking*—to allow you to activate a social media presence when the time is right. Do you really want to be Jane-Citizen1957ab, rather than Jane Citizen?

Defensive: parody, spoofs, impersonation and digital hijacking

A defensive strategy needs to recognise several areas of vulnerability.

Parody and spoofs

Social media is rife with spoofs and parodies—some hilarious, others malicious. There's no one 'right' way to respond to these; indeed some people believe parody is an important part of a healthy democracy.

Spoof accounts gain loyal followings and are so highly valued that platforms have developed guidelines for how to properly manage them. I love the colour good parody adds to online life, like the funny extrovert at the office who can lift the mood of everyone around them.

@LordVoldemort7, named for the infamous Dark Lord of Harry Potter fame, has over two million followers and makes characteristically sardonic observations, such as his Christmas 2013 message: *Santa was a Hufflepuff.* Harmless social commentary.

Professionally you need to guard against parody that makes you look out of touch or allows others to influence your reputation negatively. Parody may not be malicious but it can be inconvenient or damaging.

For example, in my home state of Victoria in 2013 during a leadership crisis the then Premier, Ted Baillieu, unexpectedly resigned. His successor, @DenisNapthineMP, declared on

Twitter: 'at least I'm not burdened by high expectations'. The announcement was made by a fake account, 'not currently the Member for South West Coast in the Victorian Parliament and Premier of Victoria'. It was the last thing a party knee deep in crisis needed. A political party is a brand. Securing the names and titles of party representatives as though they were business trademarks could have prevented it. When I last checked, the not-member account had been suspended.

But legitimate news outlets had tried to communicate with the new Premier through the account (figure 7.1).

Figure 7.1: Twitter user alerts news outlet to fake account

Andrew Lund 🐦
@andrew_lund
Hey @7NewsMelbourne heads up team @DenisNapthineMP is a fake account. Try @Vic_Premier Cheers
29 Mar

Ironically, many spoofs backfire when traditional media outlets think they are legitimate sources. Even established, well-regarded media outlets sometimes get it wrong. Both CNN and *The Huffington Post* reported stories based on tweets from a fake North Carolina Governor. The spoofer used the blunder as an opportunity to reinforce the importance of source checking (figure 7.2).

Figure 7.2: fake @GovBevPerdue uses her account to reinforce the importance of source checking by journalists

Bev Perdue 🐦
@GovBevPerdue
Don't feel bad @HuffingtonPost! CNN apparently doesn't fact check their news sources either!
6:31am - 15 May 2012

British news anchor Jon Snow fell for a fake tweet claiming CNN host Piers Morgan had been suspended. With the growing use of social media we will likely see more such spoofs in future.

Impersonation

Many platforms go to some lengths to distinguish spoofs from impersonation. Twitter guidelines state: 'You may not impersonate others through the Twitter service in a manner that does or is intended to mislead, confuse, or deceive others'. The guidelines emphasise that spoof accounts 'should not be the exact name of the account subject without some other distinguishing word, such as "not," "fake," or "fan." The bio should include a statement to distinguish it from the account subject, such as "This is a parody," "This is a fan page," "Parody Account," "Fan Account," "Role-playing Account," or "This is not affiliated with…"'

Done well, it's like the daily cartoon in a traditional newspaper. With over a million followers, Elizabeth Windsor @Queen_ UK (FICTIONAL/SATIRE) ticks all the boxes. The account transparently states it is fictional and the tweets are often clever and in good taste (as the Queen herself would be) (figure 7.3).

Figure 7.3: the nicely managed fictional Queen account

Elizabeth Windsor 🐦
@Queen_UK
Summoned Alastair Cook to Buckingham Palace after losing one's #Ashes **bet with** @Coral. #Ad pic.twitter.com/eFkDzD3Sxl
8h

Dennis Does Cricket 🐦
@FreedmanDennis
This is why we love **@Queen_UK**
#Ashes pic.twitter.com/p8IHPiMwqu
11h

There are different views on how to deal with impersonation. Some people are happy to let parody accounts run alongside their own and consider them a compliment.

If a business is being spoofed there may be legal issues to consider. In some countries you have to actively protect a trademark from being misused. I've heard numerous stories from colleagues whose organisations were impersonated where a simple tweet or call to the offender about trademark violation, rather than any hardline legal tactics, resolved the issue. I'm sure this is not always the case, but it's a good starting strategy.

Social media platforms have processes in place to deal with violations. On Twitter brand mark and trademark complaints, breach of privacy, copyright complaints, impersonation and name squatting are all violations of its terms and can be reported. Twitter also allows you to verify that you are who you say you are if your account is at risk of being parodied (in other words, you're pretty important), although this service is not available to the general public. Facebook allows users to verify accounts. But a verified account distinguishes a real from a fake account, which means you need an account to compare it with in the first place. Twitter and Instagram only accept violation reports from people who are signed up.

There are legal channels to deal with practically any online issue, but prevention is easier and cheaper. This is a fast-evolving space; both users and platforms are constantly adapting as we learn more about how people behave online.

Hijacking

The now notorious hijacking of the corporate Twitter account of UK music retailer HMV by sacked employees in 2013 reinforces that corporate accounts require controls, manageable through dashboards like HootSuite, SocialOomph and Sprout Social, to name a few. In this case sacked employees briefly took over the company's Twitter account and posted several frustrated messages before the company regained control and deleted them (figure 7.4, overleaf).

Figure 7.4: tweets from the hijacked @hmv account

hmv 🐦
@hmvtweets
Just overheard our Marketing Director (he's staying, folks) ask "How do I shut down Twitter?" #hmvXFactorFiring
1m

---

hmv 🐦
@hmvtweets
So really, what have we to lose? It's been a pleasure folks! Best wishes to you all!
11m

---

hmv 🐦
@hmvtweets
Sorry we've been quiet for so long. Under contract, we've been unable to say a word, or -more importantly - tell the truth #hmvXFactorFiring
14m

---

hmv 🐦
@hmvtweets
Especially since these accounts were set up by an intern (unpaid, technically illegal) two years ago.
14m

---

hmv 🐦
@hmvtweets
There are over 60 of us being fired at once! Mass execution, of loyal employees who love the brand. #hmvXFactorFiring
15m

---

hmv 🐦
@hmvtweets
We're tweeting live from HR where we're all being fired! Exciting!! #hmvXFactorFiring
16m

Figure 7.4: *(cont'd)*

> **hmv** 🐦
> @hmvtweets
> ...and those hard working individuals, who wanted to make hmv great again, have mostly been fired, there seemed no other choice.
> 16m
>
> **hmv** 🐦
> @hmvtweets
> Under usual circumstances, we'd never dare do such a thing as this. However, when the company you dearly love is being ruined...
> 17m

Do marketing directors need to know how to shut platforms down? It should be an essential part of corporate governance practice.

So yes, it does take time to go to each social media platform and sign up, especially if you have to do so more than once to secure a variation of your name. It can be even more frustrating if a platform allows only one account per email address. Who needs yet another password to remember? But it's pain for gain.

You can also create email aliases, for example on Gmail by putting characters behind a plus (+) sign after your username. For example, my gmail address is dionne@dionnekasianlew.com. I can create dionne+twitter1@dionnekasianlew.com. I only recently found out about this and wish I had known years ago.

Online reputation management

Online reputation management (ORM) is such a big deal that it's earned its own acronym, surely a sign that it has come of age.

There are two ways to approach ORM:

- *proactively*—generating high-value content and search results
- *reactively*—managing negative comments.

Both are important, and you need a fully integrated digital and social media ecosystem to do either. You have an online reputation, whether or not you're aware of it and whether or not you like it; it's yours to manage.

Proactively

Social media builds online reputation. When you engage and comment on content, conversations are associated with your profiles, which helps you rank higher in search engines. When someone searches for you, which everyone is doing to everyone else, they find topics and people you're associated with.

Reactively

It goes without saying that businesses must be in social networks to manage customer angst. A negative comment is an opportunity to build a relationship with someone by sorting things out. As in real life, so too in the online world.

'What if someone says something bad about us?' I often hear executives say. Well, if they are upset with you, you can bet they're already doing it. That conversation just goes on in your absence. A social presence gives you the chance to chime in. 'I'm sorry, we did get it wrong that time. This is how we're going to fix it.' The customer is not always right, and being in social is not about mass apology but about listening, gaining insights, taking the right action in each case and bringing all of that back to business strategy.

That's not new. Every day professionals face difficult situations and make decisions to deal with them. People are entitled to their own view, including about us, but that's different from damaging misinformation, in particular if it's done to hurt us. Misinformation needs to be corrected. Sometimes people online vent and move on. At other times it goes deeper and you need to take action. These are judgement calls.

Although creating and sharing original content—content marketing—is one of the most powerful ways to build your personal, professional or business brand, you have a day job. That's why I am going to teach you to curate and share others' content and use social media for ORM.

Forward-looking: activate a social media presence when the time is right for you

Finally, owning digital and social media assets puts you in the right place to go social when you're ready.

Learning by doing is the most effective way to understand the power of social media, but you can start by listening and watching. Having said that, if someone says hi because the algorithms in their digital ecosystem have found you, think about saying hello back.

Social media is not pyramid selling, where everyone you meet is a potential buyer for a cleaning product and those who aren't interested are dispensed with quickly. There are professional benefits that flow from relationships with influencers, but there are also just so many people who are interesting and worth knowing. I constantly connect online and in real life with people who have nothing to do with my work, simply because we stumble upon one another and find one another interesting. This is part of its magic.

Over-sharing and the future of reputation

Finally, an issue I know is on the mind of many is over-sharing and how it impacts people down the line. It comes up so often when I coach board directors or senior executives, or just in general conversation, that I decided to cover it here. It goes something like this.

Millennials are digital natives familiar and confident with technology. Combine this with the rise of big data (everything we do is stored), the current trend for over-sharing, behavioural traits associated with adolescence (risk taking, short-termism) and the relative newness of social media (it is yet to have its Three Mile Island, so to speak), and many fear the online behaviour of Millennials will have a negative impact in the future, including on career prospects.

My view is that, as with any period of dramatic social change, they are all growing up in the same boat. We're in this boat too. There may be some intergenerational prejudice by those who control access to jobs for graduates, but let's look at this in context.

Were you from an era of thick-framed spectacles and Harry Highpants? Did you wear bell-bottoms or kaftans? Has your long hair continued to haunt you as you moved through university into professional life? I hope not.

We may look back and blush at photographs of our hippy heyday of Cuban heels and headbands, but we should no more condemn them than those of us in nappies. They mark our progress though different behavioural phases. We can look at them and say, *that was appropriate for my age then and the time I was in*. Then move on.

Remember too that as this issue plays out it will have relevance to billions of people, not just outliers. Let's hope that compels us to deal with it sensibly. For those in positions of power who have to weigh up the enormous amounts of data on prospects it's healthy to focus on their legitimate skills, acceptable behaviours and potential, over youthful 'mistakes'.

We should also be cautious of throwing stones. Technology is creating unprecedented levels of interconnectedness and though there are many positives, there will be unintended consequences. For example, as the Internet of Things continues to grow and products become interconnected, I will be able to step on a scale and automatically share my weight with a select group on Facebook.

If I am doing the Michelle Bridges 12-week fitness program I may feel motivated by the support I receive. But how would I feel if my health insurer accessed it? Could it be used against me? We are thinking through the legal and policy issues associated with advances after the fact. The creation of a technology drives us to think about the policy, not the reverse. This will happen more, not less, as the speed of technological innovation increases.

Don't forget that data scraping, cookie tracking and breaches of user privacy by technology companies, governments and others mean that a lot of personal information about you is already out there. This is not about whether there are sordid details that might appear on the web. Comments like 'If you don't do anything wrong you have nothing to worry about' miss the point that your life is your business, not that of others, provided you are not doing harm or acting illegally.

Recruiters, for example, use search to find out details about prospects. This is legitimate. But you may not want them to know your age or that you're a single parent or that you need monthly dialysis, because these don't impact your ability to do the role well. Many biases are unconscious and can prejudice people even if they are unaware of it; ageism is a classic example. This assumes there aren't any deliberately nasty people out there who want to harm you. There are countless stories of aggrieved ex-employees or spouses who have sought to damage reputations not for legitimate, well-founded reasons but because it satisfied a darker emotional need.

Professional privacy

So does moving online mean you have to give up privacy?

There are mixed views on this. Many would say that if you've used email or text (unless you had your own servers) the question is moot, since all of that information is already stored.

As far back as 2010 technology heavy-hitters like Eric Schmidt (Chairman, Google) and Mark Zuckerberg (CEO, Facebook) declared that privacy was dead. Many people assumed we should accept this as a baseline from which to go forward.

Many large technology companies have breached users' privacy and are being sued. Some have also been compelled by law to provide details of users to security agencies or courts.

But users are saying that's not good enough.

We're at the start rather than the end of the privacy debate. Privacy advocates like Mark Weinstein argue that social media companies can be profitable without resorting to data scraping or tracking cookies. He says people should be able to be sociable while still retaining their privacy. I agree with him that these are not mutually exclusive ideas. Just because you want to reach out to someone in Alaska you find interesting, it does not mean you've agreed to become a public commodity.

Minding your Ps and Qs is important in real life and online. Use good judgement. Professionals should respect boundaries around what's commercially confidential as well as what's socially acceptable. This has nothing to do with technology but everything to do with human behaviour.

Chapter summary

Securing your digital and social media assets is vital for managing online crises and to prevent parodies and spoofs.

A strong, engaged online presence will help you to be found by search engines and to build your reputation as an engaged professional or business.

CHAPTER 8

Set the bar: social media benchmarks

People like benchmarks—they're a way of assessing where we are. Usually we do this through an annual performance review or other indicators (such as a bonus).

If you think about the performance measures you use at work, you know they're impacted by memory, bias, prejudice, personal opinion, relationships, politics and even the mood of the person doing the assessment. But they're still useful as a guide, for example on where to spend training dollars.

As in real life, so in the online world, the tools here provide useful and imperfect insights on influence. Therefore as part of establishing your Professional Platform I want you to benchmark your online influence scores. You will probably enjoy the sense of satisfaction when you come back a year later and see how much you've progressed.

There are hundreds of online analytics tools that can tell you everything from how a keyword you used in a tweet resonated with communities to how your blog ranks worldwide. But this is not a path for us. It's technical and can be overwhelming. Digital marketers, communicators, or customer and community managers should use them.

The measures we'll use are:

- Klout—which ranks you between 1 and 100 for how much influence you have on social media

- Kred—which measures the likelihood that someone trusts and will act on your posts, as well as how much you reach out to others.

Klout and Kred offer 'social proof' about your standing online. They should not, however, be your only consideration. As ZDNet's Paul Greenberg says, influence is a complex subject and not just about digital participation. Word-of-mouth recommendations and prior success on projects are enormously valuable. Having said that, some recruiters are listing a credible Klout score as essential for job applications.

Best-selling author and partner at Future Workplace, Jeanne Meister, says employers are using Klout to distinguish candidates while also taking into account the size and quality of their LinkedIn and Twitter communities. She says a Klout score will soon be a 'measurable currency'. That said, *Forbes* writer Anthony Wing Kosner says Klout can be a, 'blunt instrument, and as such, dangerous in the wrong hands'.

There's an additional reason influence measures are important right now. Many people are appending 'social media' to their résumés as a skill. Some are even advertising themselves as social media coaches without being on the platforms or knowing how to use them. Influence measures are a quick and easy way to do quick (if imperfect) due diligence. A client was recently offered Twitter training, but a quick search revealed that the coach had 100 followers and had only ever tweeted links (called link posting) of content from her website, rather than engaging or sharing the valuable content of others, including her clients. These feeds are rarely successful in the long run because they don't generate engagement. To be fair, many people who are new to social media start out posting this way until they learn the ropes.

It's important to know what online scores represent.

We're used to thinking of excellence as 90 per cent and above (or whatever your subjective figure is). But *The Wall Street Journal* (Asia) has a Klout score of 68. That puts 'must have Klout 35 and above' in a whole new context. Rupert Murdoch is known by most people around the world and has a Klout score of 91. Charlene Li from Altimer Group has a score of 78. You probably don't know her but active social media users closely follow Li and Principal at Altimer Group, Brian Solis.

When looking at Kred you need to identify what communities they are influential in. A top 1 per cent Kred in Comedian communities is not going to nail the finance role you have in mind.

Despite their flaws, it's important to be open-minded about emerging social rating systems as they have emerging value. Lithium Technologies, renowned for its high-quality social metric analytics, recently acquired Klout. Social influence and social influence measures are sure to evolve as digital life does.

Klout: the standard for influence

To use Klout go to Klout.com and sign in with Twitter or Facebook. If you don't yet have either of these, complete this after we've worked through those platforms. Then authorise Klout to use your various social accounts, for example Twitter, Facebook, Linkedin.

Once signed up, pick a number of topics that reflect your expertise. If a topic doesn't precisely fit, look for the closest alternative.

One downside of Klout is that it can be gamed by tech-savvy people who know how to set up automation, but the company is continually evolving its algorithm to prevent it (so they tell us).

Many big brands use Klout Perks to find influencers in particular target markets and then ask them to be broadcasters for products or services within online communities. In return these people are offered Kred Perks that reward them.

Klout only accesses public data so hidden social media networks are not counted towards your score (http://klout.com/corp/perks).

Kred: a transparent influence measure

Go to Kred.com and sign in using Twitter or Facebook. Then authorise the application to access your social networks.

Kred measures energy in as well as energy out—I like that. It looks at who you influence and who influences you, if your material is trusted and shared, but also what you share. Many people use social media to talk about themselves. As in real life, so too online, it's boring. The ethos of rewarding generosity aligns with my values. You get a score for Influence out of 1000 and another for Outreach out of 12. These are your Kredentials.

Kred tracks communities, hashtags and topics that are important to you, and you can use it as a navigation tool.

Tools for measuring influence

I've heard great things about Peer Index too but I've chosen to show you Klout and Kred because between them they offer you the insights you need. But there are a large number of tools that measure influence, and with growing need and uptake new products are constantly being developed. I mention them so that you know they are out there. The list is not exhaustive.

- Kred
- Klout

- Peer Index delves deeper into industry-specific authorities by identifying opinion leaders in a particular niche.

- Hubspot's Marketing Grader assesses your website and social media reach, engagement and optimisation for web and mobile.

- Crowdbooster provides analytics for Twitter and Facebook, and how to boost Twitter impact by maximising who you tweet to and when. It also generates a report on your most influential followers.

- TwentyFeet allows you to see how your key performance indicators develop over time.

- Google+ Ripples helps you assess your influence on Google Plus.

- Empire Avenue rewards users with virtual currency for activity online and ranks influencers inside and outside the community.

- Postrank calculates overall social influence and connects companies with bloggers and publishers who are influential within their communities or niche.

- Backtype shows the social impact of a URL from a blog.

Chapter summary

Klout and Kred are instruments to measure influence in an online world. They're not the only ones but for executives they're worth knowing about. By benchmarking where you are now you'll be able to see how you progress as your Professional Platform develops. Used in conjunction with other measures, they can help you distinguish genuine from fictional online expertise. Given you will not scam these systems to artificially raise your scores, they will provide a longitudinal benchmark of your social presence and are recommended as part of your basic social toolkit.

CHAPTER 9

Twitter: the global brain index

You once went to a library that used the Dewey Decimal System, first on catalogue cards and then in digital databases, to locate information that you could later discuss with family, friends and colleagues. Now you tweet on a topic and then comments and links, including to unpublished research or world-leading experts on that subject, flood in. Not only that, they continue to flow in in real-time, faster than any news service. Twitter is a powerful indexing system for the global brain.

A Twitter snapshot

It's	a microblog
Started	2006
Current number of users	nearly 300 million active but over 645 million registered users (http://www .statisticbrain.com/twitter-statistics/)
Important because	indexing system for global brain
Worrying because	trolls, fakes and people who just post links

As in real life, so online. There's a reason I've put Twitter up front in the how-to section of this book. If you decide to learn to use only one social media network in addition to LinkedIn, this should be it. (Not that I suggest you restrict yourself to one; the ecosystem is what generates the best results, but I'm being practical.)

Twitter is by far my favourite platform and the one I believe is best suited to executives. Twitter puts you at the wheel. You can listen passively or actively, participate a little or a lot. Twitter connects you to news, companies, people who share your values and interests, and cutting-edge information and ideas—all in real time. Better still, you can curate what you want to see, cutting out unwanted clutter from sources you're not interested in. If you want to hear only about 3D printing, then limit your search to #3Dprinting, although I recommend you work in 'planned randomness' because digital serendipity—or the happy accidents that result from algorithms and being online—is one of the richest unintended consequences of modern connectivity.

You wouldn't know all this from the outside, though.

To the uninitiated, Twitter looks like gobbledegook. What are these short bursts of text with incomprehensible combinations of letters like *shar.es/Uce3E*? What are these half conversations full of @ buttons and #hashtags? Combine these mysteries with the fact that you tend to hear about Twitter in the media only when something has gone wrong (which accounts for only a fraction of the Twitter stream) and I can understand why you might be a little wary about stepping in. But with a little insight, and Twitter is easy to learn, you may come to think about it differently and even, like many executives, learn to love it.

The backstory

So what is this thing called Twitter and how did it come to play such a central role in contemporary communication?

Put simply, Twitter is like texting, only doing so very publicly—in fact on a global scale. You publish a short text and it goes out on your feed for the world to see, share or respond to.

Because Twitter allows you to share only 140 characters at a time, a tweet, it is called a microblog (small blog). But it's also a social network because those tweets are shareable. Within the 140-character bursts is a rich narrative of shared data, articles, research. There's also a history of long, deep, shared conversations and the evolution of communities. Although only the most recent exchange is readily visible, if you click Expand the full history is revealed. For that reason Twitter is often regarded as an information network—its utility has gone far beyond what was originally anticipated.

To me, Twitter is like an index for the global brain, or even a circuit of it. Twitter processes billions of bites of information and synthesises them into an important but imperfect representation of reality, much like the brain does.

Created in 2006 by Jack Dorsey, Evan Williams, Biz Stone and Noah Glass, by 2012 Twitter already had 500 million registered users posting 340 million tweets per day, and it's popularity hasn't slowed down. Twitter is now one of the 10 most visited websites in the world and handles around 1.6 billion search queries daily. And it's still growing. (By the way, if you want to know how a website ranks then you can use a measure such as Amazon's Alexa.)

Like most platforms, Twitter has continued to evolve and become more sophisticated as it has learned what users want. In 2011 it enabled people to share photos, and later the app Vine allowed users to create and share six-second looping video clips.

Although founder Jack Dorsey says the Twitter name came from its eponymous definition as 'a short burst of inconsequential information', it has ended up as anything but.

A single tweet can destabilise the stock market or locate a kidney donor for a patient, break news or connect someone with an idea to someone who can help make it a reality.

Remember the library

Do you remember the first time you went to a library? All those books! No one would have expected you to walk straight in and locate that precious copy of *Green Eggs and Ham* or whatever you were into at the time. You would not have taken a quick look around and stormed out, declaring libraries a waste of time, and actively tried to dissuade others from using them. Everyone knew you had to learn how to use the catalogue. There was a librarian to help but once you knew the system you could use it to source any information you liked.

That's Twitter. The only difference is you're familiar with libraries and that makes them easier to accept. Many people glance randomly at a feed of tweets, have little idea what the characters mean and, finding no personal relevance, declare it a waste of time. Know how to use it, though, and it's one of the fastest ways to find quality information. And not just information but those who are producing, sharing and talking about it and making decisions about how it will be used.

But it goes deeper than that. Twitter can take you from abstract curiosity to a discussion about emerging research before it's formally published. You can find an angel investor for a project, contribute to discussions, connect people with one other, and be part of many borderless collaborations for pleasure or profit, or both.

You can also develop new relationships with those who share interests and who, without the benefit of Twitter's algorithms, you would never have known existed. While some of these may remain virtual connections, many will cross over into real life or, where geography restricts it, find their way onto Google Plus hangouts or Skype.

When used well, the power of Twitter to connect you with exciting, innovative and engaging information, thinking and people is unparalleled.

A Twitter case study: bringing ideas to life

I could pick any of thousands of case studies about how effective Twitter is (for just about anything), but let me focus on one my favourite projects of 2013, the #superawesomemicroproject. From go to whoa everything about this project involves a combination of random and planned connections of people in social media networks to bring about something of potentially great value to the world.

The #superawesomemicroproject was born when Romanian technology genius Raul Oaida sent Australian entrepreneur and marketer Steve Sammartino (@sammartino) a message on LinkedIn looking for someone to back an unusual idea—a car made of Lego that ran entirely on air.

Fortunately Sammartino is the kind of guy who is open to random connections and interested in how technology brings people together and ideas to fruition. He dived in.

He issued a single tweet asking for backers to contribute between $500 and $1000 to fund the project, clearly stating that there would be no fiscal return on the investment and that it was high risk and could fail. That's openness. It didn't stop 40 Australian backers from hopping on board, another benefit of global collaboration, which distributes risk. With enough money to fund the half million Lego pieces, the car was built in Romania and moved to Melbourne.

The finished product was unveiled via social media in December 2013. Compressed air, stored in two small tanks, was released into a pneumatic engine, which turned the car's drive shaft, and off it went. It worked. The test drive made global news and the YouTube video quickly climbed to over a million views, and by the time this book went to print it had reached almost five million views.

The Lego hot rod is a stunning example of how social media brings together people and ideas that can do good in the world, and of the critical role of Twitter in funding and socialising the project.

Twitter for professional development

To stretch the library analogy, Twitter is something akin to having the best set of encyclopedias on your shelves, only imagine them as alive, up to date and willing to speak when you ask them a question.

Twitter's generous, intelligent users are contributing to the emergence of a global brain. Many are happy to share their expertise and views on topics, from research and technology to science, psychology and art and beyond. There is no limit. Twitter and other social media creates abundance, you need to understand this to appreciate the value.

This information is still available in journals and books, but Twitter gives you direct access to the people who are writing for them, while they're doing it or even before they've started. It works both ways. Many authors will say that comments from the community influenced their thinking and the ability to directly 'ping' a fan and let them know you've got something out creates a virtuous circle of readership and sales. Lady Gaga asked her 41 million followers which of her new studio tracks they liked most and then released it on iTunes within days—effectively creating a multimillion dollar tweet. Twitter means business.

You can tweet a question: *What do you mean?* Or *I would like to know more, please recommend links.* Or just follow what they are saying and take advantage of what they are sharing, shortcutting the junk to valuable content. At what other time in history have we been able to ask the smartest people on Earth about their views and ideas—and regularly get an answer?

For professionals and businesses, it's a goldmine.

Business embraces Twitter

Look at some of the companies tweeting up-to-the-minute research findings and opinion. I've included their Twitter handles and their own bios to show you how the 140-character limit can be used with great effect.

- *@eMarketer.* The World's Go-To Source for Information on Digital Marketing, Media and Commerce.

- *@BCG.* The Boston Consulting Group is a global management consulting firm and a world leader on business strategy. Find new research on @BCGPerspectives.

- *@McKQuarterly.* The business journal of @McKinsey & Company. Our goal is to offer new ways of thinking about management in the private, public and nonprofit sector.

- *@Accenture.* Follow us for updates on Accenture research, blogs, podcasts and more. Tweets by the Accenture Twitter Team.

- *@Capgemini.* People matter, results count.

- *@Deloitte.* Share the latest news, research, events and more from Deloitte Touche Tohmatsu Limited (DTTL) and Deloitte member firms.

- *@forrester.* Forrester Research, Inc. is an independent research company that provides pragmatic and forward-thinking advice to global leaders in business and technology.

- *@Nielsen.* Global consumer and media insights from Nielsen.

- *@IDC.* The premier global provider of market intelligence, advisory services, and events for the IT, telecommunications and consumer technology markets.

- *@ExactTarget.* ExactTarget is a leading global provider of cross-channel interactive marketing SaaS solutions across email, mobile, social and websites.

- *@BoozAllen.* Provides management and tech consulting to the US government in defence, intelligence and civil markets, and to major corporations, institutions and nonprofit orgs.

- *@KPMG.* Driving a conversation on emerging business issues and opportunities. Follow our tweets from around the globe at http://www.kpmg.com/twitter.

Figure 9.1 illustrates how big companies verify accounts and secure the many variations of their names.

Figure 9.1: McKinsey accounts highlighting different business areas

McKinsey & Company 🐦
@McKinsey
Since 1926, the trusted advisor to the world's leading businesses, governments & institutions I 100+ offices in 50+ countries I Knowledge
@McKQuarterly

McKinsey Global Inst 🐦
@McKinsey_MGI
The business and economics research arm of McKinsey & Company, covering topics such as economic growth, capital markets, technology trends, and urbanization.

McKinsey Mktg&Sales 🐦
@McK_MktgSales
McKinsey on Marketing & Sales: We help clients deliver above-market growth by improving and connecting capabilities across the entire organization.

McKinsey on Society 🐦
@McKinseySociety
McKinsey & Company's Social Sector Office - seeing, hearing, spreading ideas on social impact in education, economic development, sustainability & global health

McKinsey on BT 🐦
@mck_biztech
Official updates from the Business Technology office of @McKinsey. (Founded May 2008) Curated by @cbarthold

McKinsey China 🐦
@McKinseyChina
Ruminations & research on China from McKinsey & Company. Curated by @GlennLeibowitz. Subscribe to the McKinsey on China podcast on iTunes:
itunes.apple.com/podcast/mckins...

McKinsey is a great example of a company that has secured handles for the global corporate, then various product segments (allowing them to target specific audiences), right down to showcasing the expertise of employees in their global network.

- *McKinsey_MGI.* The business and economics research arm of McKinsey & Company, covering topics such as economic growth, capital markets, technology trends and urbanisation.

- *@McKinseySociety.* McKinsey & Company's Social Sector Office — seeing, hearing, spreading ideas on social impact in education, economic development, sustainability and global health.

- *@McKQuarterly.* The business journal of @McKinsey & Company. Our goal is to offer new ways of thinking about management in the private, public and nonprofit sector.

- *McKinsey on BT.* @mck_biztech. Official updates from the Business Technology Office of @McKinsey. (Founded May 2008. Curated by @cbarthold.)

They have a list of employees who use Twitter (figure 9.2) and it's publicly available for those who want to subscribe — great social practice in transparency, openness and adding a human element to a brand (https://twitter.com/mck_biztech/lists/mckinsey-on-twitter).

Figure 9.2: public list by McKinsey of its people on Twitter

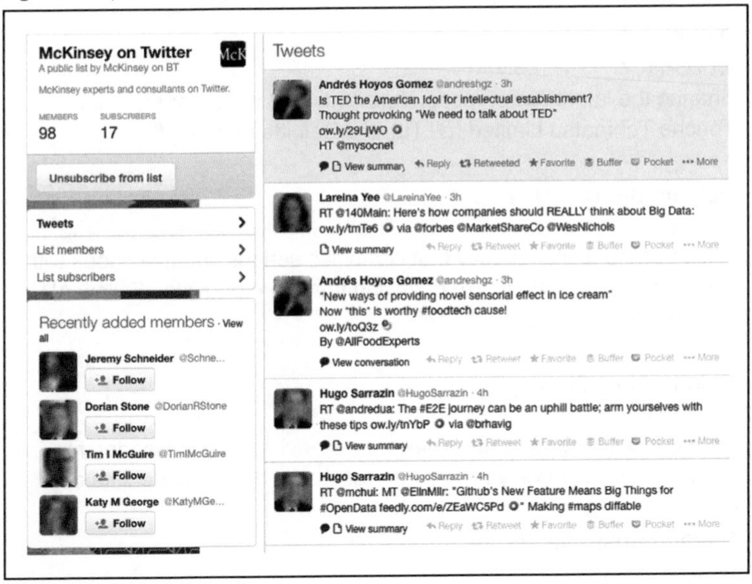

For businesses still worried about opening up social media to their employees, this shows how doing so can create a wonderful synergy between corporate and personal professional use. Conditions of use can be set out in governance policies and employment contracts.

Obviously I can cite only limited examples. My point is to demonstrate by way of offering reassurance and examples you can relate to large, global companies with the same concerns about privacy, security and reputation management as you are highly social.

Figure 9.3 (overleaf) illustrates the range of Deloitte services.

Figure 9.3: consultancies that have created a broad social net

---

Deloitte 🐦
@Deloitte
Sharing the latest news, research, events and more from Deloitte Touche Tohmatsu Limited (DTTL) and Deloitte member firms.

Deloitte Digital AU 🐦
@DeloitteDIGI_AU
A full-service digital agency that combines serious creative chops with trusted business sense. We're driving the future of digital. Follow AU updates here.

Deloitte Univ Press 🐦
@DU_Press
Where ideas prosper. Latest news, #research & thought leadership from Deloitte University Press. For questions: dupress@deloitte.com

---

Deloitte Australia 🐦
@Green_Dot
Recognised for our innovation, our seven signals and our commitment to the reinvention of professional services. You can also hear from us at @AuDeloittian

---

Deloitte UK 🐦
@DeloitteUK
Latest news & research from the business advisory firm Deloitte UK. Deloitte UK refers to Deloitte LLP, UK member firm of DTTL
deloitte.co.uk/about

Deloitte Tech 🐦
@DeloitteOnTech
Your source of news and information from Deloitte LLP on Emerging Technologies.

Figure 9.3: *(cont'd)*

PwC US Fin Services 🐦
@PwC_US_FinSrvcs
Follow us for insights about issues affecting US financial services
organizations across banking and capital markets, insurance, asset
management & real estate.

PwC_sustainability 🐦
@PwCclimateready
Making business and economic sense of sustainability

PwC Malaysia 🐦
@PwC_Malaysia
4 time winner of Msia's 100 Leading Graduate Employers Award.
Follow us 4 industry-related news & resources, or download our free
app: bit.ly/iiz3sO

PwC_Digital 🐦
@PwC_digital
Digital is more than the latest shiny thing. It's about outcomes -
customer experience, enabling mobile payments or even eliminating
gov't service silos.

PwC New Zealand 🐦
@PwC_NZ
The most important thing we do is build relationships with our clients
and people. We're committed to delivering quality assurance, tax and
advisory services.

PwC Industry/Geo PR 🐦
@PwCIndustryPR
Laura Schooler, PwC US PR Director. Follow for insights & info
impacting major business industries and U.S. geo markets.

(continued)

Figure 9.3: consultancies that have created a broad social net *(cont'd)*

BostonConsultingGrp 🐦
@BCG
The Boston Consulting Group (BCG) is a global management consulting firm & the world's leader on business strategy. Find new research on @BCGPerspectives.

bcg.perspectives 🐦
@BCGPerspectives
bcg.perspectives, produced by The Boston Consulting Group (@BCG), delivers cutting-edge thinking on business & management issues.

BCG_Consultant 🐦
@BCG_Consultant
Insights from a 2nd year consultant at The Boston Consulting Group, based in San Francisco. Views are my own. For official BCG news & information, follow @BCG.

BCG_Associate 🐦
@BCG_Associate
Insights from a 2nd year associate at The Boston Consulting Group, based in Boston/Hong Kong. Views are my own. For official BCG news & information, follow @BCG.

BCG on TMT 🐦
@BCG_TMT
News and insight from the Technology, Media and Telecoms Practice of The Boston Consulting Group (@BCG)

It's not just that these brands are there to link you to their products. They are regularly posting high-quality, free content that helps you to do your job better.

Figure 9.4 shows some tweets on a list I built for businesses that do online research. All the links to articles are free and you'll see immediately that they are highly relevant.

Figure 9.4: list of online research with high-quality links

Nick Bilton 🐦
@nickbilton
Entering the Era of Private and Semi-Anonymous Apps:
bits.blogs.nytimes.com/2014/02/07/ent...
Feb 8

Capgemini 🐦
@Capgemini
Digital Transformation: A CEO Imperative... featuring
@capgeminiconsul via @melrossdigital: ow.ly/to4AS
Feb 8

Deloitte US 🐦
@DeloitteUS
What Maytag didn't do that Heartland did: Followed #TheThreeRules
#tedxtalks spr.ly/6013eCPX
Feb 8

Capgemini 🐦
@Capgemini
64% of respondents to a recent @capgeminiconsul & #MIT survey
said the pace of #tech change in their orgs is too slow ow.ly/tdSqB
Feb 8

Deloitte 🐦
@Deloitte
Deloitte taps into big data to help member firm clients gain business
insights, deliver innovative solutions #GR2013 ow.ly/qKPAi
Feb 8

eMarketer 🐦
@eMarketer
MINI USA's @leenadler cautions against focus on short-term sales
goals when evaluating real-time programs ow.ly/to3kM
Feb 8

Later I will show you how to set up lists that curate your interests specifically for your business or industry and to increase your influence. You can go straight to these lists each day and cut through the noise to get straight to the heart of what matters to you. You can keep your interests narrowly focused on professional and business interests or go wide.

In figure 9.5, which lists some of my favourite Twitter accounts, you'll see a skew towards personal passions (science, psychology, art, technology, social media), but you can build them around any topic you like. It's like browsing through a library shelf full of books on a topic you're interested in.

My Twitter list Must Read Everyday (publicly available from my Twitter page https://twitter.com/DionneLew/lists/must-read-everyday) is a go-to place for me the moment I hop online. You will most likely find a multitude of carefully curated public Twitter lists on your key topics of interest.

From my list I can see at a glance what's happening across the world on issues that affect me professionally in leadership, technology and social media. Personally I find it's a great way to start the day, but it also allows me to point people to information I know they will value. My capacity to do this grows the more people I meet online. And it doesn't always have to be about the latest research.

Figure 9.5: personally curated, public Twitter list

GOOD 🐦
@GOOD
Want to make your city more spontaneous? Join a Google Hangout w @Hunter_Franks' League of Creative Interventionists: ow.ly/tmTc3
2h

Medium 🐦
@Medium
"You Can Already Code - You Just Don't Know It Yet" by @edrex_ medium.com/p/862044601a5a..
2h

Open Culture 🐦
@openculture
Häxan, 1992 Horror Film Narrated by William S. Burroughs: cultr.me/ 10fpUwU Added to our list of 625 Free Movies cultr.me/17g6npO
2h

Alice Bell 🐦
@alicebell
"We have seen exceptional weather. It is consistent with what we might expect from climate change." telegraph.co.uk/topics/weather..
2h

LiveScience 🐦
@LiveScience
To the Powerless, World Weighs Heavier dlvr.it/4tbHR0
3h

Slate 🐦
@Slate
Oh No, Russia's New Olympic Darling Skates to the Theme from Schindler's List slate.me/1f4OcAZ
3h

Co.Design 🐦
@FastCoDesign
Infographic: The worst place to live in the U.S. if you hate crappy weather. f-
3h

For example, I made a connection with a social media consultant specialising in crisis management through Twitter. Given we are both Melburnians we consolidated the connection over coffees. I learned a lot about the role of social media in defence, but also that she was a Buddhist and a passionate fan of *Game of Thrones*. When Mashable announced Season Four of *Game of Thrones* was previewing on Vine I pinged her instantly. This is the human side of social media. You get to know people, their interests and likes and connect around them much as you would in real life. It's a natural extension of who we are day to day.

Some of the world's best-known intellectuals use Twitter. I have placed them in a list I call Edge Types (https://twitter .com/DionneLew/lists/edge-types) (figure 9.6), after John Brockman's @edge, because I am a huge fan of his annual book, a collation of short essays by great thinkers around a particular topic. These are people who make me think.

Here, for example, you'll find:

- world-leading astrophysicist Neil deGrasse Tyson @neiltyson tweeting links to podcasts on cosmic queries or making jokes
- Professor Dan Gilbert @DanTGilbert riffing on psychology
- MIT Professor and Chief Scientist Sinan Aral @sinanaral talking about social media, big data, networks and what's happening around the digital world.

Figure 9.6: feeds from Edge.org writers who tweet

These are very visible thought leaders but there are many other interesting thinkers and mavericks who provide a constant challenge to the status quo.

Do these people tweet back?

I recently saw an event at the Royal Society that I wished I could attend but thought would also appeal to @create_discover, someone in Manchester in the UK with whom I regularly engage. Quantum physicist @jimalkhalili joined in the conversation to let me know he would be coming to Melbourne (figure 9.7, overleaf).

Figure 9.7: random connections generating valuable links across geographies

---

Dionne Kasian-Lew 🐦
@DionneLew
@create_discover @jimalkhalili @royalsociety so much going on over there you have amazing access to great speakers -
Jan 23

Paolo Feroleto 🐦
@create_discover
@DionneLew @jimalkhalili @royalsociety Come and join us, the weather's great!
Jan 23

Dionne Kasian-Lew 🐦
@DionneLew
@create_discover @jimalkhalili @royalsociety never been in April
Jan 23

Jim Al-Khalili 🐦
@jimalkhalili
@DionneLew depends if you're coming for Bill Bryson or me. I'll be visiting and speaking in Melbourne in early May.
Jan 23

Dionne Kasian-Lew 🐦
@DionneLew
@jimalkhalili Oh wow fantastic - can you send a link please?
Jan 24

Jim Al-Khalili 🐦
@jimalkhalili
@DionneLew will tweet when I know more details.
Jan 24

Dionne Kasian-Lew 🐦
@DionneLew
@jimalkhalili that would be excellent - hope you have some time to explore our wonderful laneway culture
Jan 24

This 'random richness' happens all the time in social media networks and in business too.

CEO of DOMO Josh James believes CEOs who shun social media risk losing touch with lucrative customers, prospects and influencers. He describes how Twitter was instrumental in the establishment of his business:

> For anyone doubting the benefits of a CEO's presence on Twitter, I can vouch for its impact. Being on Twitter is generating a steady flow of inbound customer leads, partnership introductions and quality recruits for my business data startup Domo.

Twitter is being used effectively for business and in marketing. This isn't a social marketing book so I won't go into that in detail, but I will mention hashtag campaigns because you've probably heard about them in particular, when they backfire. The amplifying effect of negativity is not just the hallmark of modern media (which thrives on conflict) but deeply human; our fondness for sharing bad news goes back a long way. However, hashtag campaigns can be very successful if they are useful to the people they are targeting.

Three examples of hashtag campaigns

Consumer: In the UK Domino's Pizza cut the price of a Pepperoni Passion Pizza (say that fast 10 times) by one pence each time someone tweeted #letsdolunch. After 85 000 tweets the price dropped from £15.99 to £7.74, and Domino's offered that price from 11 am to 3 pm that day. It worked.

Political: In 2011 the Obama administration used social media to personalise a payroll tax debate by tweeting 'What does #40dollars mean to you?' The $40 was what workers would lose on average if Republicans ended the payroll tax cut that was being debated. Making it personal and speaking directly to voters got more than 17 000 people responding (remember, this was 2011 and it was about tax), and that affected the outcome of the debate.

Sport: In 2010 the Australian Football League's Carlton Football Club used the believe hashtag to expand its fan base and grow membership numbers by directly engaging its fans for ideas.

Social issues

Twitter has been criticised for an inability to do justice to complex social issues with its information soundbites and fast-moving feed, and even for generating online negativity. But Twitter is not a replacement for conversation; it's a part of it and a link to more detailed analysis elsewhere.

Those who thrive on being offensive and stirring negative emotion don't typically sit down to read a 10-page analysis that challenges their beliefs. Although social media broadcasts are uncensored and immediate, we're used to negativity from years of print, radio and TV. That doesn't make it right—just the same old same old, amplified.

Twitter can also be used constructively to raise awareness. For example, a London blogger started the #ididnotreport hashtag after reading a story on how few victims reported assault crimes for fear of not being believed. The hashtag prompted broad discussion and led to the emergence of a new and positive #webelieveyou hashtag to support those who were speaking out.

These moments in time are not the beginning and end of an issue, just as raising difficult issues in real life does not resolve them overnight. That is an oversimplification, and life is complex. Business is complex. Communication is central to both. And the way we do that has evolved.

Twitter shot to mainstream fame when it became the first place that news of the 2008 Mumbai bombing was shared. Twitter had only six million members at the time, but eyewitnesses used it to post around 70 tweets a second, which were shared around the world.

Although these social media users were instrumental in sharing breaking news about the incident, their role evolved as the crisis unfolded. Soon they were using Twitter to plead for blood donors to head to the hospital, to share details of hotlines so people knew how to get in contact with authorities, or to get messages to family and friends that they were alive.

Twitter was only one of many new media platforms used to share information. Within a few minutes of the attacks a new page was set up on Wikipedia, with a team of citizen editors providing real-time information. Vinukumar Ranganathan also uploaded 112 photos to Flickr (at the time you could not share photos directly on Twitter).

Twitter was so little known that the Indian government considered shutting it down to prevent terrorists from accessing too much detail about what was going on. Now law enforcers use it as a powerful tool to gather the collective intelligence of citizens and try to prevent harm.

If this was the first time that Twitter morphed from social media network to newswire, it would not be the last. There have since been thousands of examples of Twitter being used as the major communications channel during crises such as floods, fires, earthquakes and other disruptive events. Journalists, news organisations, law enforcers and emergency services now consider Twitter central to emergency and disaster management.

It was a very different ball game, for example, during the Boston Marathon bombings in April 2013, when Twitter was used to announce breaking news, report updates as facts were verified, counter misinformation, circulate images of the suspects and, ultimately, announce their capture.

Twitter and the Boston bombing

Barely seconds after the bombs exploded during the Boston marathon, tweets started flooding the internet. The

#bostonmarathon hashtag quickly became established, as did others like #bostonstrong and #prayforboston.

Many local journalists who had been running in the marathon were able to live-tweet from the scene. Incoming feeds from journalists were monitored through tools such as TweetDeck and the *Boston Globe* newspaper downloaded these straight to its live blog. That enabled readers to get the latest consolidated information on the disaster as it was happening from multiple sources. Journalists also harvested tweets from citizens for news that they could subsequently verify and publish.

The Boston Police actively used Twitter, from the first tweet (seeking video of the finish line—figure 9.8) to the last (announcing the capture of the suspects). The first tweet was quickly retweeted over 3000 times.

Figure 9.8: the Boston Police's first tweet after the bombing

Cheryl Fiandaca 🐦
@CherylFiandaca
Boston Police looking for video of the finish line #tweetfromthebeat

Related headlines
Boston Marathon blasts: three dead and more than 100 injured – as I... The Guardian @guardian
Cops use Facebook, Twitter, YouTube to catch perps
NBC Investigations @NBCInvestigates

Police also put out an alert to the community to assist them in identifying the suspect (figure 9.9).

Figure 9.9: the Boston Police's community alert

Boston Police Dept. 🐦
@bostonpolice
Do you know these individuals? Contact boston@ic.fbi.gov or 1-800-CALL-FBI (1-800-225-5324), prompt #3
pic.twitter.com/QJias1Kywe

Many newspapers embedded the tweets directly into their reporting. Finally when suspect Dzhokhar Tsarnaev was apprehended, that was tweeted too (figure 9.10).

Figure 9.10: further post-bombing tweets by the Boston Police

Boston Police Dept. 🐦
@bostonpolice
Suspect in custody. Officers sweeping the area. Stand by for further info.

Related headlines
Boston bombings: 'CAPTURED!!! The hunt is over,' police say
CNN @CNN
April 19 Updates on Aftermath of Boston Marathon Explosions
NYTimes Lede Blog @thelede
Second Bombing Suspect Alive and In Custody
People magazine @peoplemag

Not surprisingly the last announcement was retweeted widely (137 882 retweets and 46 614 favourites).

These organisations were able to swing instantly into action because they owned their Twitter accounts and already had established followings. Companies must own Twitter accounts if they are going to deal with an online crisis where it happens — online.

Of course, the power of Twitter to spread information quickly also means it can be hijacked for nefarious purposes, and there were those who quickly hopped online to set up accounts just so they could do so. After the Boston bombings a detailed report was published analysing the amount of real versus fake content during the event.

Researchers examined the 20 most popular of the 3.7 million users who tweeted about the event. Because I am not a professional researcher, I will leave those who are to decide how good the research methodology was; it's the principle rather than detail that is of interest here.

What the researchers found was that much of the commentary that came from these accounts was of the unremarkable, 'our hearts go out' sort. Unremarkable perhaps, but predictable and very human. Twitter is communication and not every tweet aims to serve up a hard-hitting fact, any more than every conversation does. It simply does not work that way.

The researchers found that 29 per cent of tweets contained fake information or rumours that were subsequently shared. (This again is nothing new if you think about how readily people share unsubstantiated gossip.) The writers were interested in whether algorithms could be built to detect and manage this kind of fakery. Although it is not immediately apparent how this can be done, the research showed that the reputation and impact of a user (social reputation, global engagement and likeability—the influence measures we were talking about earlier) can in part predict how popular a tweet is. Having a verified Twitter presence with a credible reputation is a no-brainer. Credible sources have always been highly valued. You've got to put yourself in the picture.

People will also try to abuse the need for quick information and exploit panic. For example, in Boston between 15 and 20 April nearly 32 000 new accounts were created to tweet about the bombings. Two months later Twitter suspended almost 20 per cent of those for bad behaviour. Some tried to imitate legitimate profiles (which is why securing a handle as part of a defensive strategy is wise). Fraudsters who seek to capitalise on others' misfortune in times of crisis—are there echoes here of looting during a flood? The dark side of social media is not about social media, it's about human nature. But we need to understand the particular permutations it takes online so we can manage it.

Which brings us to an ugly topic.

Trolls

There's always a bad egg. Do you remember how people used to say that in the 'good old days'? The squeaky wheel that got the oil? Well, nothing has changed and trolls still get a fair share of attention—only, like all things relating to social media, their effect is amplified.

Let's look at a horrible example, one I think encouraged many professionals on the verge of poking their heads out to close the door again. The only silver lining in this tale is that users sent Twitter a very clear message: if we're going to be there, ensure that we are safe.

Caroline Criado-Perez, a writer and strong believer in human rights, lobbied the Bank of England to use the image of British author Jane Austen on the back of the new £10 note when it was next updated. So she was delighted when the bank confirmed that Austen would replace Darwin in 2017, but her pleasure would quickly turn to something quite different—fear.

No sooner had the announcement been made than Criado-Perez found herself on the receiving end of a sustained and coordinated campaign of abuse on Twitter that included horrific death and rape threats. She was not alone. Women and men who tried to push back against the online aggression became targets. Within days 9000 people had signed an online petition calling for Twitter to add an abuse button for those threatened with sexual violence and to make the site responsible for any criminal threats posted on it. Rape threats are a criminal offence, whether they happen in real life or online. And those trolls were subsequently approached by the police.

Learning by doing: Twitter 101

Now head to Twitter.com and sign up. Figure 9.11 shows the sign-up page.

Figure 9.11: Twitter's sign-up page

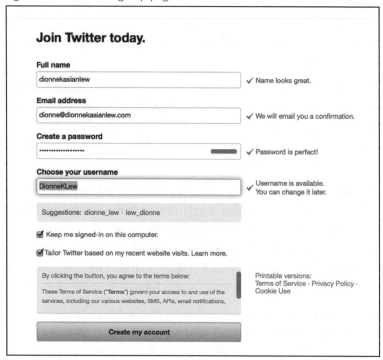

Twitter will send you an email verifying that you have set up an account and offering some suggestions for who you might want to follow. If you go back to your email, you will see the email with suggestions similar to figure 9.12.

Figure 9.12: Twitter will offer prompts of people to follow

You can also keep progressing your setup from the last screen (figure 9.13).

Figure 9.13: Twitter prompt screen

Click Next. This is where you build your timeline.

Who to follow

You will need to follow five people. Twitter uses algorithms. That means you teach Twitter about your interests and it will use what it knows about these to bring people and information to you that are pertinent. While you can just randomly follow people to get started now, with a view to teaching Twitter later, there's a benefit to choosing real interests from the outset, because Twitter will immediately start to offer suggestions. You can follow:

- people you know—either you'll already know their twitter handles or you can search for them on Twitter

- topics that interest you—searching by using hashtags such as #socialmedia, #CEO, #corpgov or #sustainability

- businesses or companies that interest you—such as some of those I mention above.

You can also search for users by location, which means Twitter locates people in that area for you.

I am also going to show how to use hashtags that relate to social media for executives to show you how this influences the suggestions Twitter makes—I suggest you use ones that relate to your own interests.

You will see that Twitter immediately delivers four suggestions that relate directly to what I am looking for, providing me with people and businesses that have 'socialCEO' in their title or that tweet about the issue (figure 9.14). Follow them all.

This is a less common search so Twitter has provided me with only four options. But for broad topics such as 'business', many more would have been delivered. As you can see in figure 9.15, the suggestions I follow appear immediately on the right-hand side of my timeline. I search for #socialbiz and follow the additional suggestions that Twitter makes.

Figure 9.14: search results using #socialCEO hashtag

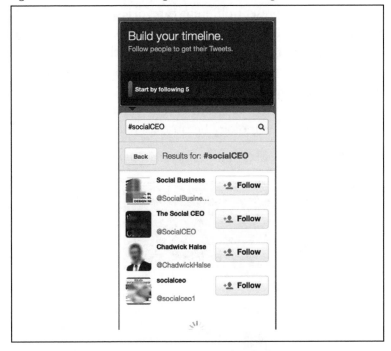

Figure 9.15: search results using #socialbiz hashtag

Click Next. Twitter will again prompt you to follow more options and will present different categories such as news, TV, music, sports and other topics. Feel free to add in whatever interests you. You'll see that Twitter has worked out from my IP address that I am Australian and that local angle is reflected in the suggestions on Politics, bringing up accounts for the current Australian Prime Minister and other politicians. I am going to choose Technology because it's relevant (figure 9.16).

Figure 9.16: screen showing Twitter suggestions for who to follow

Once you've done this, Twitter will prompt you one last time. Here you may choose to give it permission to enter your email account and search contact lists to make suggestions. Whether you want to authorise this is up to you. If not, simply continue the process of adding keywords.

If you allow Twitter to access email contacts it could help your follower process by giving you heaps more people to connect with. However, you may not want to do that for privacy reasons, in which case you can just select another five users. I am going to add @McKinsey because I know they have at least five accounts I can tick and I'm interested in what they publish. Finally we're in and can start developing your profile.

Your profile

Your Twitter account is part of your digital footprint. That means it has to reflect who you are. So there is no single or right way to brand accounts. We start with the 'Add character' screen (figure 9.17).

Figure 9.17: screen for photo upload

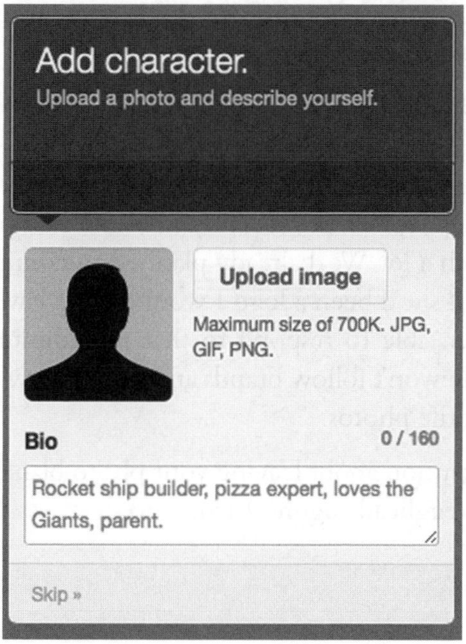

There are countless articles on social media and branding that offer advice on when and when not to use photos and logos, how people respond to avatars ... the list goes on. Your comfort levels will also play a role. I too have a view, but I will keep my advice short, simple and unscientific.

Use a nice, recent close-up photograph of the real you. There are many reasons for this, not least that others will be able to identify you across the digital universe and if you decide to connect over Skype or in person. It's about continuity. It's also important to be authentic. Unless you're a zany, out-there, larger-than-life character, a headshot of you with mouth agape and eyes crossed is not going to work. Blurry says 'I don't care'. It seems unnecessary to point out that the image should not be provocative, but I do so because a very senior executive I know recently told me he refused an invite from a high-level recruiter to connect because her look was more dating site than professional network.

Some corporates like to use brand logos. I think this works well if you allow your people to be social, as in some of the examples above. Personally I prefer photos — they help you get to know people. I was recently in a café and saw a woman I engage with a lot. We'd already planned to connect later that month, but if she'd been a logo I would never have recognised her and been able to respond to that serendipitous meeting. Some people won't follow brands and only follow people with 'normal' profile photos.

A word of caution about leaving your photo blank: it will turn you into an egghead (figure 9.18).

Figure 9.18: a Twitter 'egghead'

And that's an absolute no-no. Most people I know don't like eggheads because they don't have any idea of the person who sits behind them. Yes of course you can cheat and put up a photograph of someone else, but we are talking about how normal people use Twitter, not the con artists. Moreover, the bots I am going to teach you to use to clear out fake followers or spam identify eggheads as possible spam.

Your bio

This is your 160-character opportunity to tell people who you are and what you stand for. Don't confuse being professional with being bland. Inject some personality, but keep it real.

If you have more than one account it's good to signal it so people don't become confused if they stumble across you somewhere else. For example, professionally I am @dionnelew but I also write a personal blog at @beyourwholeself, and I make sure that they reference each other. I'll talk about managing dual accounts a little later.

Add words that your users might search for in your bio with the appropriate hashtag: *If you're big on #sustainability be nice to see it there.* If you're a Non-Executive Director there's a whole community of #NED who will know how to find you by that hashtag.

The anatomy of Twitter

Now you're up and running, let me show you around. We'll start on the left side of the screen and work our way towards the right. As you can see from the setup screen I am following 19 people and I have one follower; so far I have not sent any tweets. This is my Home page, which is what you will see when you first open Twitter up.

On the left you can see four key tabs—Home, Notifications, Discover and Me. You will know which section you are in because it is highlighted. Here we are in the Home section (figure 9.19).

Figure 9.19: Twitter Home page menu options

Home

Your open Home page looks like figure 9.20. We will get to the options on the right in a moment; for now this is where you search, find direct messages (DM), adjust settings and compose tweets.

Figure 9.20: Twitter Home page

Home displays the stream of tweets from users that you follow. The more people you follow the more tweets there will be, which means after a while flicking through these tweets to look for good content is going to become impractical. Still, if you want to see everything that everyone you follow is saying, go take a look. What's going to be far more important, though, is using search to find people or topics directly and building lists.

Connect

Connect is the business back end of Twitter—it's where all the action happens. Nobody but you can see this part of your Twitter account (figure 9.21, overleaf). On the other hand, everything you publish appears under Me and is visible to all.

Figure 9.21: Twitter interactions

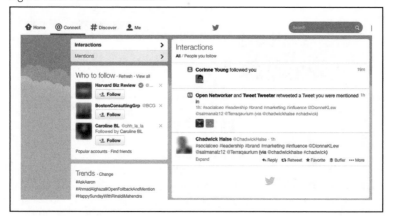

When you click on this section you will see two options on the left—Interactions and Mentions (figure 9.22).

Figure 9.22: the two screen options

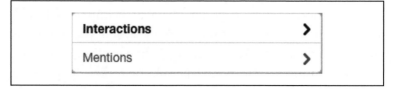

Interactions

If someone wants to let you know they are speaking about you they will mention you by your Twitter handle, which always has @ in front of it. Whatever has been sent to you will appear here. That means if at 3.00 am somewhere across the world a follower wants to send a message or share a link you will find it the next time you tune in to this part of your account. If you think about it, how else would you know that someone had sent you a message? There are 500 million tweets a day floating around out there. The equivalent is your email inbox.

Twitter also uses this to let you know who is following you. I can see that even in the process of setting up this account I have gained a follower, someone I know personally who follows me on @dionnelew. That's because Twitter lets followers know when someone they might know comes on board.

Mentions

Mentions directly shows messages sent by one person to another.

When a person sends a tweet with an @mention in it people can see it in their feed. Until you 'do' something with this mention, it won't appear publicly in your Twitter stream. It sits there like a piece of opened email, waiting for you to decide what you want to do with it. You can ignore it, delete it or respond to it—whichever you wish. But remember that once you reply it will alert the person you mention and appear publicly on your feed.

Discover

There are, as I have said, some 500 million tweets a day; these are like books in a library in that while each may be important to someone, they're irrelevant to you unless you're looking for that information. That's where hashtags come in. They allow you to search for information by topic.

Say I want to talk about the Boston bombings. Every time I tweet I will add the hashtag #bostonbombing, which adds my tweet to the pile. People who are looking for information on what's happening can search under this hashtag, and everything that's been posted on it by anyone who is talking about it—not just people you know—comes up.

This makes hashtags both an important discovery tool and also a way to connect with people you don't know who share an interest. For example, I have a strong interest in leadership and when I post new content I add the #leadership to my tweets. That way everyone in the leadership community who is searching for information under that tag can find it, read it, share it, send it out into the Twitterverse. And each time you tweet it will show your face (or logo or avatar, depending on how you have set up your profile) with your little message. You can delete a tweet and it will disappear from your account as well as that of the person you sent it to—unless it's been shared further. The exception is a retweet, which we will get to in a moment. The other thing to know about a retweet is that it doesn't show your face, but rather the face of the person you have retweeted (figure 9.23).

Figure 9.23: a retweet shows the profile picture of the person you are retweeting

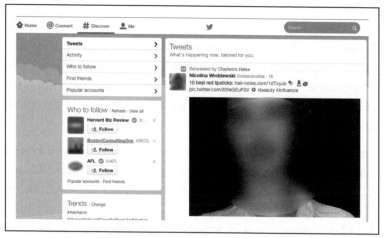

In Discover you can look at tweets but also any of the following menu options (figure 9.24).

Figure 9.24: menu options in the Discover section of Twitter

Me

Me is pretty self-explanatory. You can see your profile and bio, a summary of the tweets you've sent, your followers and who you are following. There's also a menu that allows you to look at your tweets, following, followers, favourites and lists (figure 9.25).

Figure 9.25: menu for the Me section of Twitter

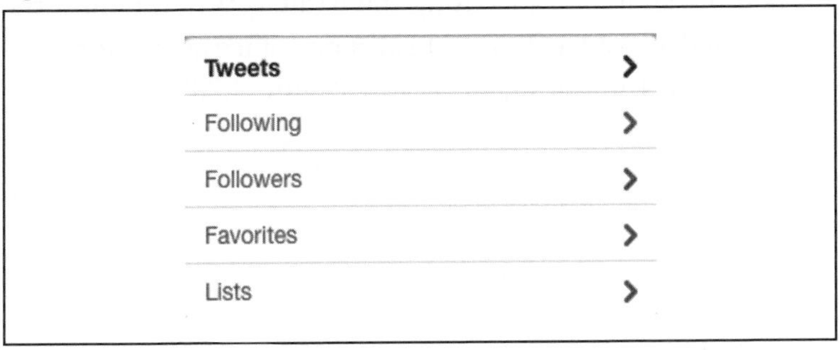

Lists are very important for professionals, as I have said, and we will build some shortly.

On the right side of your Home page you'll see four icons (figure 9.26).

Figure 9.26: Home page icons

Search

You can search for a person using the @ symbol before their name. For example, I am searching for author @mikemyatt. Twitter gives me two options and I can go into each to look for the Mike Myatt I want (figure 9.27).

Figure 9.27: how to search people

I can also search by topic, using the hashtag. When I enter the #socialmedia hashtag Twitter brings up topics (at the top) and accounts that I might like to follow (figure 9.28).

Figure 9.28: how to search topics

Direct mail looks like a little inbox.

This is the direct message section of your account. The messages exchanged here do not appear publicly. Still, always be cautious about what you share. I have known many a person to think they're sending a private message, only to discover they have sent it around the world because they mistakenly sent it as a tweet.

It's useful, though. If you're heading out to catch up with someone you can alert them if you're running late. That's not necessarily a conversation other people will be interested in so it's better pushed out of public view, where it would only create more noise. There's no rule about that, however.

Settings

Settings are found behind the little cog icon (figure 9.29).

Figure 9.29: the settings icon

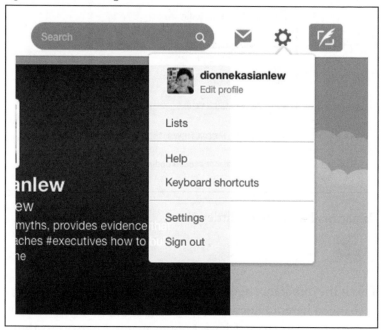

Multiple options will appear when you open Settings.

- *Account details.* These will have been filled out during the setup process. If you need to make changes—you've moved to another country, say—choose the location and press Save at the bottom of the screen (figure 9.30).

Figure 9.30: where to find account settings

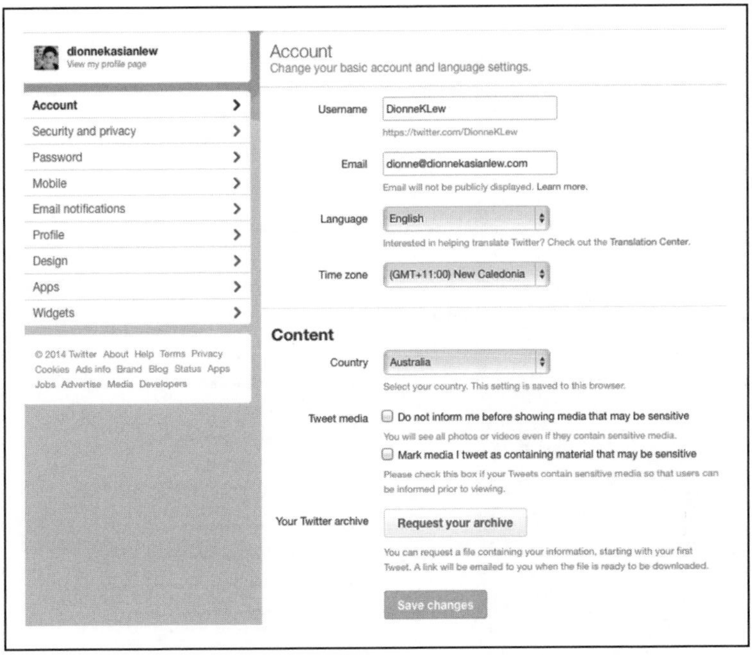

- *Security and privacy.* You can set your security to verify login requests and to require personal information if you reset your password (figure 9.31, overleaf). I always choose the highest security option. If you want to protect your tweets tick the box in privacy, this means your tweets will not be publicly visible. Only people who you approve can read your tweet stream. I don't see the point but understand, for example, that some project teams like to use Twitter in this way.

Figure 9.31: where to find security and privacy settings

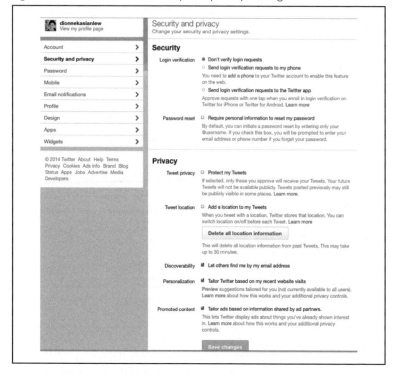

- *Password.* You can change your password here (figure 9.32).

Figure 9.32: password and verification settings

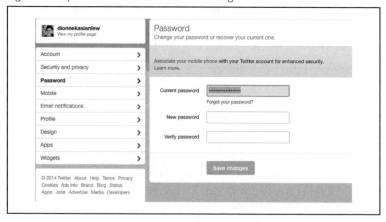

- *Mobile.* The best place to use Twitter is on mobile. The apps allow you to manage your platform on the go wherever you are. If you click the mobile app link it will give you the option of downloading Twitter for Android or iPhone (figure 9.33). You can also do this by going to the App Store direct from your mobile.

Figure 9.33: adding a mobile phone

- *Email notifications.* If you leave these ticked your inbox will fill up very quickly. I untick them all (figure 9.34).

Figure 9.34: unticking email notification boxes

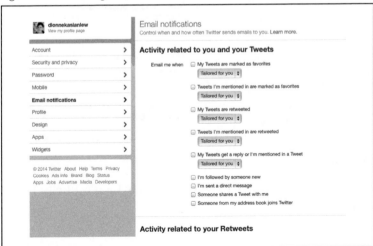

- *Profile.* Here you can provide more detail on who you are and where you live. Add in your location details and a website link. If you don't have a website add the URL for your About.Me page or LinkedIn account. I have used my LinkedIn account in this example. I don't link my Facebook account because, as you'll learn, I keep my Facebook private, but if you want to connect them, just push the icon and follow the prompts (figure 9.35).

Figure 9.35: profile settings

Design

You can choose a pre-set Twitter theme, which is fine to begin with (figure 9.36).

Figure 9.36: design settings

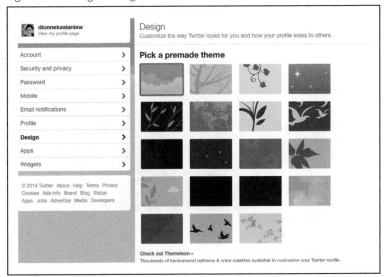

Preferably, though, customise your site to make it stand out. If you're a thought leader, represent your message in some way. You can upload a background image. If you have a logo or corporate colour, use it. If you don't then choose something that you believe reflects who you are. I can't overstate the importance of design for professionals. Arriving at a site that is scrappy and unkempt sends a message that you don't care. Regardless of where I source design I have found it to be expensive. Consider it an investment. You can create an image file and upload it and adjust the background and link colours so they coordinate with your new background image. You will need the hex codes for the colours in your image if you want the background and links to match. Google 'hex colour codes' and you'll find lots of sites that provide this information (figure 9.37, overleaf).

Figure 9.37: the Quick Online Color Picker Tool

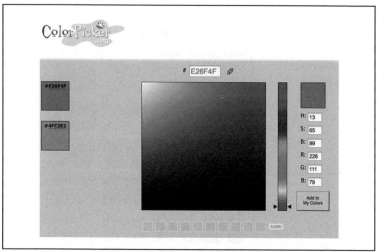

Add a background image and change the background colour and link colour to whatever you have selected. Remember to press Save (figure 9.38).

Figure 9.38: customising design settings

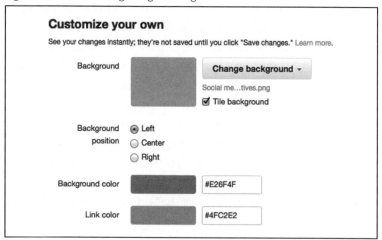

Now you have a personally branded Twitter page and are ready to learn to tweet, share, retweet and build influence (figure 9.39).

Figure 9.39: a branded Twitter account

No apps or widgets will be showing at this stage because you have not added any, but this is where you will see any apps you have given permission to access your Twitter account (you can revoke access by following the prompts).

Build a following

Who you follow and why is highly personal. Some people only follow friends. Others only follow people who share their interests. Mostly people follow anyone who follows them provided they're not spam, fake accounts, trolls and so forth. That's my approach. How you decide, though, depends on what you want to get out of it.

For example, I am an author and a consultant. I want the largest audience with an interest in my work to read it and share it. This is because I hope the content will be useful to them, but it's good for my profile and my business too. However, and you will hear me say this time and time again, I believe in going outside your square. So I like to engage with fellow artists, swap recipes, get involved with projects.

Following someone means that each time they post something it appears on your Twitter Home page. Updates for the people you follow appear in reverse chronological order with the most recent update on top of the page. The more you follow people the less that matters because you don't depend on chronology to find information—you depend on search.

There are several strategies for building a following:

1   Follow people and companies of interest. Just search by @ or # to find them. Because I am interested in social media law I have selected @SocialMediaLaw1 who is @GlenGilmore a Forbes Top50 Influencer Tweets≠Legal Advice.

2   Next you can go to a person or company whose tweets look valuable. Have a look at who they are following or who is following them, and follow them back (figure 9.40).

Figure 9.40: building a following by following people whose content you value

3   Invite people you're connected with on LinkedIn.

4   Allow Twitter to access your email contacts.

5   Tools like Tweepi allow you to scan the list of accounts that follow your followers so they are likely to be of interest. Just go to Tweepi.com, sign in with your Twitter account and follow the prompts.

6   Follow the accounts Twitter recommends in #Discover or 'Who to follow'.

The other vital component of building influence is to ensure you share great content regularly. So you will learn to tweet. For your Twitter account to gain traction you will need to tweet regularly, at least eight times a day.

According to Dorie Clark, author of *Reinventing You: Define Your Brand, Imagine Your Future* and a lecturer in marketing at Duke University, studies have shown that the more you tweet the more followers you have. If you've produced fewer than 1000 tweets you'll typically have fewer than 100 followers; tweet 10 000 times and you'll gain 1000–5000 followers.

Although you do need to put in effort in the startup phase, there are many tools, like Buffer and HootSuite, that will help you to schedule tweets. Because it's going to be vital to our strategy, let's set that up now. You can choose any of the scheduling services you like, but because I use Buffer I am going to use it here.

Setting up Buffer to schedule tweets

Go to Bufferapp.com and sign in with Twitter. Add in your details and create a new account (figure 9.41, overleaf).

Figure 9.41: authorisation screen

Download the extension to your web browsers. Just click Install or skip that step. You'll be prompted again later, because installing the extension allows you to save things to Buffer straight from the web browser (figure 9.42).

Figure 9.42: Buffer icon

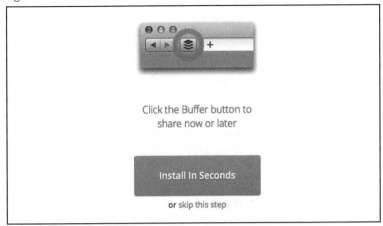

Buffer will open on your Home page. Running across the screen you will see tabs for Analytics, Schedule and Settings. Running down the left you'll see you can add social media accounts under the Connect More button. Over time you will add in LinkedIn and other accounts. Buffer allows you to share any piece of content to any of the platforms simply by ticking them (figure 9.43).

Figure 9.43: Buffer Home page

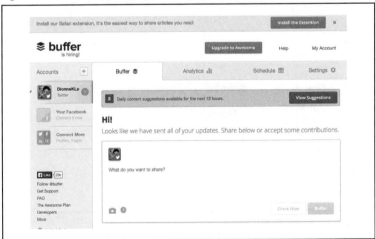

Fill in your details under My Account at top right (figure 9.44).

Figure 9.44: account settings on Buffer

You can add team members, reconnect or remove social media accounts you've added in Settings (figure 9.45).

Figure 9.45: settings on Buffer

As you haven't yet tweeted, the Analytics section will be empty.

Select Schedule (figure 9.46). Here you can select how often you want to post each day of the week. I know from experience that the number of tweets I send directly correlates to the engagement I get. I also need to reach people in different time zones so I spread my Schedule across 24 hours. On weekends I go quiet. That's my time out.

Figure 9.46: scheduling tweets on Buffer

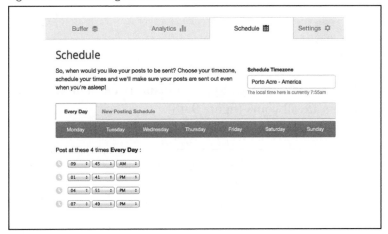

You can add team members, reconnect or remove social media accounts you've added in Settings (figure 9.47).

Figure 9.47: adding team members on Buffer

Now your Buffer is up and running, let's learn to tweet.

The anatomy of a tweet

A tweet is a text message of a maximum of 140 characters, but it's amazing what you can cram into it. In fact you will come to find that the limitation of 140 characters builds a useful discipline that increases the information density of each tweet. You'll use all of the basics we've talked about. To compose a tweet, just go to the compose tweet icon.

Clicking on this icon will open a blank tweet. The next 140 characters are all yours (figure 9.48).

Figure 9.48: composing a tweet

Including a hashtag in a tweet makes it part of a conversation on a particular topic across the web. As I have said, hasthtags are like library cards that are used to catalogue information by topic. So if I put in #socialmedia then I am sharing the link or statement I have made broadly, adding it into the pool of information on this topic. It also makes what I have said searchable. If I am looking for the latest on the #higgsboson (in physics) or what's happening at the #AustralianOpen, it helps me cut through. That means that when you tweet you want to think about what information you're sharing and how it should be catalogued. Not all tweets will contain a hashtag. For example, you tweet someone to say hello and good morning; that's a snippet of conversation but the value is in the connection, not the information.

Feel free to create your own subjects—just make sure you don't use any spaces between words. The #discover tab at the top of the page will display content and hashtags that might interest you, based on your own tweets.

Decide if you want to signal someone with your message, and if so include their @. As you get to know people you develop an understanding of their interests, and when you find a good article you may want to send it to a group of people, much as you used to do on email (figure 9.49). This allows a number of people to participate.

Figure 9.49: adding #topics and @people to tweets

You'll see that I have the option to either Tweet or Buffer the tweet I have composed. If I tweet it, it will appear immediately in Me—remember, this is my public stream (figure 9.50, overleaf).

Figure 9.50: Me screen showing public, published tweets

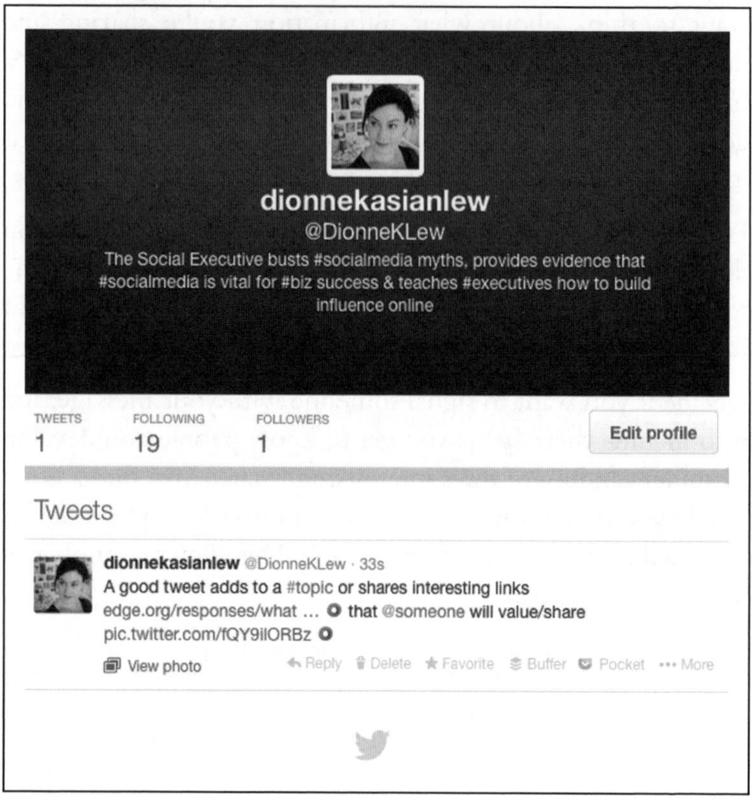

Buffer tells us that adding an image increases engagement. By performing some tests and analytics they found that:

- tweets with images received 89 per cent more favourites

- tweets with images received 18 per cent more clicks

- tweets with images received 150 per cent more retweets.

Add a photo or image by selecting the icon on the left (figure 9.51). Once you've shared an image or video, it is also displayed on your page in 'Photos and videos'.

Figure 9.51: adding a photo to a tweet

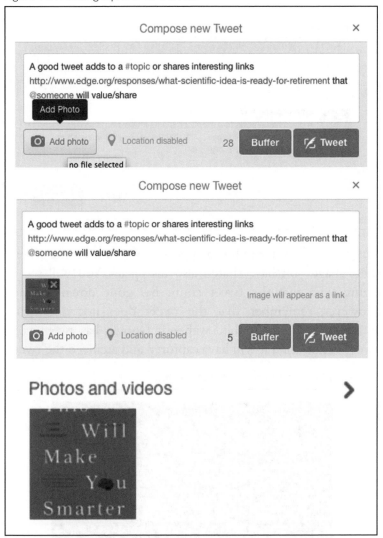

So what happens if you make a mistake and want to delete it? All you do is select the trash icon Delete at the bottom of your tweet. Press the button and it will open the tweet and allow you to delete it using the button on the right (figure 9.52, overleaf).

Figure 9.52: deleting a tweet

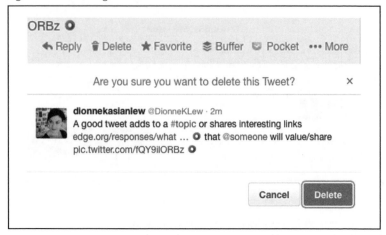

Once a tweet is deleted it disappears from your Home screen. The image you have shared also disappears. You will see in figure 9.53 that the tweet count has gone down to zero. However, remember that the tweet does not necessarily disappear from the public web—if Google has swept your tweet stream then it will have captured and archived the tweet.

Figure 9.53: Me screen shows tweet deleted

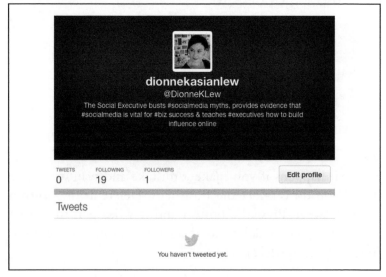

The tweet in figure 9.54 catalogues the content into #socialmedia. It provides a high-value link to Boston Consulting's report on the internet economy and attributes the source directly to @BCG. That means they'll see your mention of them in their @Notifications. I have also 'pinged' or directly signalled to @BenGilchriest, a research lead at Capgemini at the time of writing whose work I quote on digital maturity, to see if he agrees and engage him in my tweet. Questions are a great way to increase engagement but they should be used only when they fit. You can't add a question to every tweet.

Figure 9.54: building a high-value tweet for engagement

Note that I try not to use all characters allowed because I want others to share my message and add their view. This allows people to add RT (retweet) when they share my tweet. The general etiquette is to only use 120 characters to allow those who retweet your tweet to add their own comments, and hence their own value, to your tweet.

The link I have shared is long. However, I could shorten this by using bitly, ow.ly or other link shortening tools, which would also allow me to customise and track engagement with that link (figure 9.55).

Figure 9.55: published tweet in Me screen

I can either tweet immediately or push the tweet into my Buffer schedule. If I tweet immediately, it appears in Me.

I can now go back and check my @Notifications (figure 9.56). Remember this is your email box. I can see that someone has directly mentioned me. That tweet has been favourited by someone else (this is just another way to keep track of tweets you want to remember) and I have a follower.

Figure 9.56: checking interactions

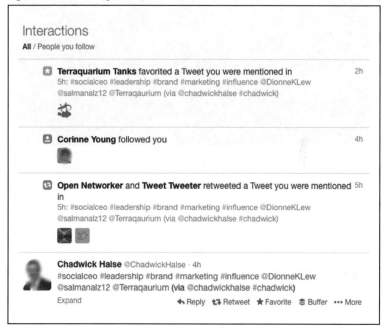

I can open up the profile of the follower and decide if I want to follow them back (figure 9.57, overleaf).

Figure 9.57: opening up the account of a follower

Just press the Follow button on the right.

Retweeting

Retweeting is a way to share something interesting with followers. When you retweet you are citing a source. Be careful what you retweet, though, because as a publisher you are responsible for what you share. Simply push the retweet button (figure 9.58). (Retwact can help manage this.)

Figure 9.58: a retweet

Because you are citing a source, that tweet will appear in Me exactly as you have tweeted it, including with the face or logo of the source (figure 9.59).

Figure 9.59: the different profile of a tweet vs retweet in Me

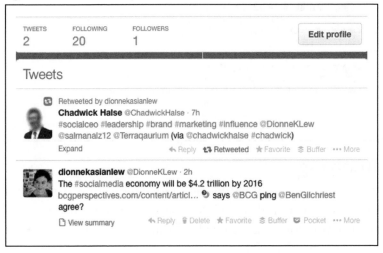

You can undo a retweet by clicking on the retweet symbol, which shows Undo Retweet (figure 9.60). However, if it's already been shared, things can get tricky. Retwact can help manage this for the last five tweets.

Figure 9.60: undoing a retweet from @Notifications

This does not mean it will be deleted from the accounts of any other Twitter users who may have shared it in the meantime.

If you want to share the information using your face or logo, then open up Buffer and select 'Change to Quote'. This will show up in your feed with your branding but using the RT to show that is a direct quote of the source (figure 9.61).

Figure 9.61: distinguishing a quoted and a retweeted tweet

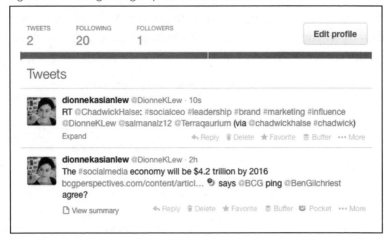

Replying

One thing you want to do each morning is look at who has mentioned you and reply. This starts to create a relationship. Clearly you don't want to reply if someone has sent something offensive, but that's rare.

Simply push reply and a screen will open under the tweet to which you're responding. This will link them into a thread going forward, which means they're always joined. I saw that a rather unusual Twitter feed that claims to be about optical illusions was included in the mention, so I have asked a question about it (figure 9.62).

Figure 9.62: replying to a tweet

If you go to Me you'll see only my reply (figure 9.63).

Figure 9.63: only my reply shows in the Me screen

But if you press View Conversation, the history will unreel (figure 9.64). This is how you make sense of conversation on Twitter. It may appear as a fragment, but behind it is a history, accessible to all. You'll see I use a conversational tone. Scripted corporate speak and spin don't work in social media. But you also don't need to be unnaturally awesome. Tweet as you would speak. At the end I've added a hashtag that expresses a sentiment rather than a topic, as I've explained. Because I mention two accounts, both of these will be notified in their @Notifications buttons that I have mentioned them. I can open and close conversations by toggling between expand and hide. This only changes the view; it does not delink them.

Figure 9.64: expanding a tweet to reveal the conversation

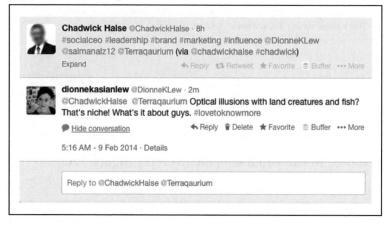

Building your Twitter influence

Now you've set up your account and learned to tweet, share and retweet content, you need to build your influence.

There are several ways to do this:

1   *Grow your following.* Tweet often, tweet good material and follow people back. Over time you will build up your following. When you approach following 2000 people, Twitter will not allow you to follow any more people until you have more followers than you are following. This barrier can be quite frustrating for Twitter users. What you need to do is to clean out followers who aren't adding value because they don't tweet or are spam or bots. I show you how to do this below. Just persist. Eventually the ratio will be right and you'll get over the hump. After that, there are no barriers.

2   *Find influencers to follow.* There are several tools to help you do this, though I have yet to use any of them. They include Radian6 Influencer Widget, Crowdbooster, Commun.it and FollowFriday Helper. I really think you get to know who matters as you tweet, and it's not always the biggest influencers. I love chatting to people with interesting views who may not have the biggest influence scores but who are engaged and interesting.

3   *Periodically do 'big follows'.* That means going to the followers of someone you admire and following those that have mutual value. However, be aware that Twitter tries to strike a balance between useful levels of automation while preventing spammers from spoiling the user experience. Following or unfollowing a large number of users in a short period of time is considered 'aggressive following' or 'follower churn' and can get you

suspended. If you get suspended from Twitter, it won't respond to requests to reinstate your account as you have to wait for the algorithms to run their course.

4   *Post great content.* I will show you how to use lists and Scoop.it to curate good content.

5   *Engage.* When someone tweets, reach out and comment on what they have shared. When someone mentions you, reply to them using the reply button.

6   *Schedule across time zones.* Use a scheduling tool.

7   *Use lists.* Lists are a powerful way to categorise people and topics, and can be private or public.

8   *Favourite a tweet.* If you see a tweet that interests you or the people who mentioned it interest you, click the star icon to Favourite that tweet. Those people will be notified. It is then likely that they will check your account and potentially interact or follow you, especially if you have already reached out to follow them.

9   *Let people find you.* In Settings allow people to find you by searching your email address or phone number. Check both options and add details. This allows others to find you more simply when they search on Twitter.

Building lists

Lists allow you to group people or topics together in any way that makes sense to you.

You can build a public list, which means anyone can view and subscribe to it. Good public lists are really useful and reduce the amount of work that others have to do to find resources. This is how people on the internet help one another without each person needing to reinvent the wheel. It's part of building the abundance of the social web.

For example, Deborah Weinstein (@debweinstein) has a great list of CEOs who tweet (figure 9.65). I stumbled across the list from this Toronto PR agency during a typically random Twitter excursion but immediately subscribed because it captured the audience I am interested in. One way the agency grows the list is to invite people to tweet suggestions to @SO_pr—another great example of online reciprocity.

Figure 9.65: public lists of CEOS who tweet

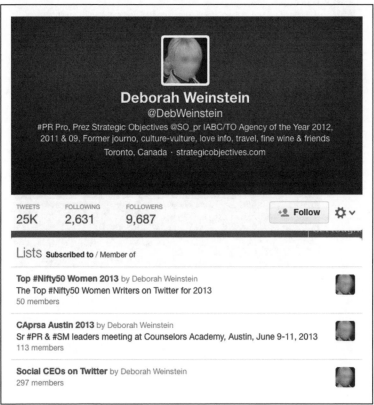

Anyone can go in and look at who they are and how they are doing it (figure 9.66).

Figure 9.66: member of a public list

To build a list simply go to the Settings icon of the Twitter account you want to add to a list. You will see a number of options, including the ability to block the user or report them for abuse and even embed their profile (figure 9.67).

Figure 9.67: list setting

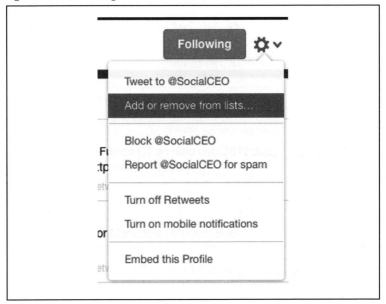

Click the 'Add or remove from lists' button (figure 9.68).

Figure 9.68: creating a list

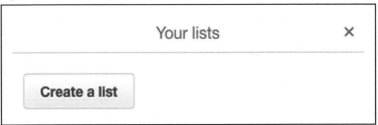

Once you press the 'Create a list' button you will be prompted to give it a name and description (figure 9.69). When the list is public a description will help others work out if it's useful to them.

Figure 9.69: naming a list

Make sure you save (figure 9.70).

Figure 9.70: saving lists

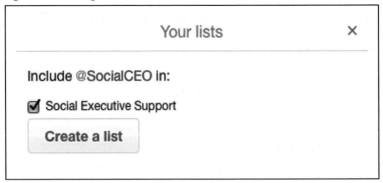

Click the 'Add or remove from lists' button. Keep adding relevant people to lists as you encounter them.

You may also want to consider building a private list, for example of people you like engaging with. If you click Private no one will see it. But it's a good prompt for you because you can go into the list and see everything your friends are sharing and engage with them, as well as being sure to share the love.

Weekly hygiene

Some people try to game Twitter to secure big followings. What they do is follow hundreds or even thousands of people, then as soon as you follow them back they unfollow you. It's a classic trick of spammers or those dodgy companies that try to sell you Twitter followers. It pollutes your platform with followers who aren't real and add no value. Buying followers will get you suspended from Twitter, never do it.

It's therefore important to see to your Twitter hygiene once a week—a bit like getting your house in order before the work week starts. I will say, though, that it takes time for people to go through and respond to new follower notifications, so don't clean up your account too soon after you've done a 'big follow' or you will not give people a chance to keep on top of their own hygiene. I usually take time on the weekends to go through new followers and follow back.

There are several tools you can use to get rid of fake followers, spam or those who are not following you back, including:

- ManageFlitter
- Tweepi
- Twit Cleaner.

Twitter has terms of service for developers that change regularly. Again Twitter is trying to strike a balance between encouraging interesting development and protecting users.

I use ManageFlitter (figure 9.71), which is why I am sharing it here, but feel free to explore.

Figure 9.71: ManageFlitter screen

Simply head over to the platform and use your Twitter account to sign in. I've used my regular account to do this (figure 9.72).

Figure 9.72: connecting using Twitter

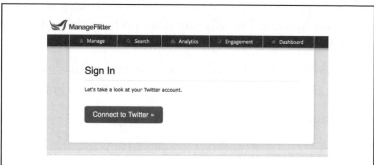

The site will go through and categorise all your followers. It will also show you when you followed them. I always start with the last pages first, because page 1 will show those I've followed most recently who may not have had time to include me.

Remember that not all businesses or celebrities follow back. If they're important to you and you want to see their content but not clog up your following list, you can add them to a list (figure 9.73).

Figure 9.73: Manage Flitter options

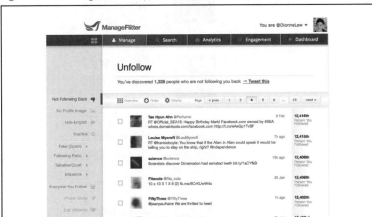

On the left, you simply mark the boxes of anyone you want to stop following (figure 9.74, overleaf).

Figure 9.74: click the box to unfollow

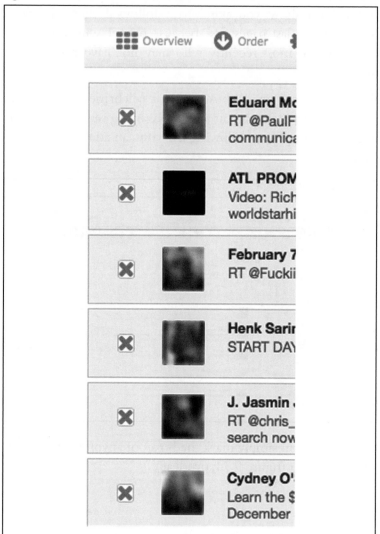

The number of accounts you tick will show on the right and you can process them by clicking Manually Process (figure 9.75).You used to be able to delete them automatically, but Twitter changed its conditions and this is the solution that Manage Flitter found. It's probably worth mentioning that platforms are constantly changing terms and conditions and the third parties that engage with them therefore have to tweak their products.

Figure 9.75: processing unfollows

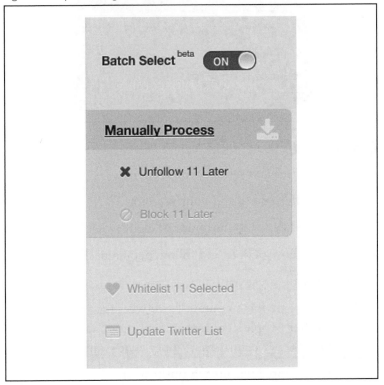

You can also click on Manage and scroll down to Process and get rid of them in this way (figure 9.76, overleaf).

Figure 9.76: another option for managing unfollows

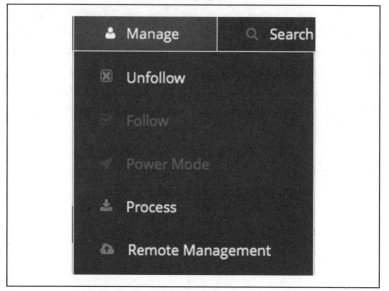

Checklist

1 Go to Twitter and set up your account.

2 Go to Buffer and set up your account.

3 Set a schedule for a minimum of eight tweets a day.

4 Start to follow people and follow people back.

5 Start sharing great content.

6 Share other people's content by retweeting or quoting it. Share other people's content in a ration of approximately 80/20 — 80 per cent theirs, 20 per cent yours.

7 Reply to people who reach out to you.

8 Build Twitter lists.

9 Leverage off the lists of others.

11 ways to increase your influence on Twitter

1   Twitalyzer helps measure engagement and reach using tracking data on Twitter. It' a pretty sophisticated measure and offers great insights for marketers, though it's probably not necessary for an executive managing a personal brand.

2   Twitter Grader measures the number of followers, the follower/ following ratio and the level of engagement from the audience out of 100, including regional or local influence levels—a nice combination.

3   Commun.it helps you get a handle on who's influential in your Twitter network.

4   Tweetlevel helps brands use Twitter effectively, and is again more for the communications and marketing area than the individual.

5   Twitaholic ranks you on Twitter by followers and by location. Be aware, though, that it's more important on Twitter to have engaged followers rather than just the numbers. There are also a lot of companies who now sell Twitter followings.

6   Twitter Counter provides statistics of Twitter usage so you can compare how other (more influential) people use the platform—a rats and stats approach.

7   Qwitter sends an email any time someone unsubscribes from your Twitter profile and mentions a possible Twitter post you made that may have caused them to leave.

8   WeFollow allows you to add yourself to a listing of Twitter users by tags you find interesting.

9   SocialOomph allows you to schedule when a tweet is posted.

10   Twitter Grader is a great service that grades any Twitter account and gives you additional details and ranking information.

11   FriendorFollow helps you to find out who's not following you back and who's unfollowing you.

Twitter rules

Here are some guidelines for engaging on Twitter:

- Share about 80 per cent of other people's content and around 20 per cent of your own.

- Mix up your photo/logo with those of others in your tweet stream, although keep it mostly about you. That makes you identifiable, but people also get a clear idea of what you write about and whether or not it's worth coming back to visit. If all people do is retweet the content of others, then their feed becomes one face or logo after another of random content. It's confusing to get a sense of the brand or person you are dealing with. As much as possible, try to think of Twitter as a conversation that's taking place in real life.

- Remember your manners — say please and thank you.

- Cite your sources.

- If there are too many people being copied in, names can end up taking up all the space, particularly if the material has been tweeted a few times. Rather than RT @nameofperson RT @nameofperson RT @nameofperson, replace all the RTs with a single MT (multitweet) and keep some of the names. The source is most important.

- If you write 'via' and an @source, it means that's the person or company who wrote the material.

- Cc means to copy someone in because you think they should see what you're sharing.

- A 'ping' (ping @soandso) is like a tap on the shoulder — you use it to tell someone directly you think the material will interest them. You will get a lot out of this.

This chapter will get you up and running on Twitter but once you've learned the ropes you may want to amp it up with some Bootcamp suggestions. These are pro tips. I've included sources for these great tips so you can look up authorities and follow their other fabulous suggestions.

Twitter bootcamp

- Never start a tweet with @mention because only people who follow you and that person will see it (Gary Vaynerchcuk). Even when replying to people about a general topic add a ".." as the first letter of the reply if you want everyone who follows you to see your reply. If you only want people who follow both you and the person to who you are replying to see your reply, then start with @mention.

- 'Use the Google Keyword Planner to find keywords that make up your industry or market … tap into existing traffic rather than generating it from scratch. It is better to know about keywords than even about hashtags, because a hashtag is a keyword or a "theme" that can help amplify your exposure.' (Ken Krogue)

- Use Tweepi to target followers. (Jeff Bullas)

- Use Hashtags.org information to improve your social media strategies.

- Tweet visual and multimedia content as this is much more shareable—tweets with images receive 150 per cent more retweets. (Courtney Seiter)

- Tweets get more traction when there's a little room to spare—shoot for 120–130 characters. (Courtney Seiter)

- Create a Twitter landing page on your website and link to it from your bio so that when you send people to your website from Twitter you thank them. (Kim Garst)

- If you're using a hashtag to join a conversation stream, be sure to use that specific hashtag—and remember, no spaces. (Rebecca Hiscott)

- Find which of your LinkedIn connections is on Twitter and follow them. First, visit your LinkedIn Contacts page and select 'Settings'. From there you'll have the option to export your contacts into a .csv file. The file can then be seamlessly uploaded to your email account contacts. Then from Twitter you'll be able to import your email contacts, which will include your LinkedIn connections, choosing which of them you want to follow. (Dorie Clark and Daniel Vahab)

Chapter summary

Twitter is like an index for the global brain, connecting you to news, companies and people who share your values and interests in real time.

Twitter plays a vital role in managing real-life crisis, not just with respect to sharing information but to tapping into citizens, to donating resources, supporting recovery efforts or even identifying suspects.

Twitter is also a business and professional development goldmine, linking you to cutting-edge information and ideas.

CHAPTER 10

Lock in LinkedIn: a new, global business lunch

As in real life, so online. You used to make connections, share expertise and get recommendations by networking. Now you connect globally through LinkedIn. It's a new, global business lunch.

A LinkedIn snapshot

It's	a business network
Started	2003
Current number of users	259 million in 20 countries
Important because	professionals connect here
Worrying because	it's been hacked

LinkedIn is like a business networking event: it's where you go to make mutually beneficial connections, share expertise and get recommendations on anything from suppliers to future talent. But signing up for LinkedIn and then not doing anything once you're there is like going to a business lunch and standing in the corner.

LinkedIn was launched in 2003 and is the thirty-sixth most visited website in the world. It's a publicly listed company with more than 259 million users from over 200 countries and is available in 20 languages. There are other professional social networks, such as Viadeo (50 million) and XING (10 million). LinkedIn penetrates around 30 per cent of the population of the US, Canada, the UK and Australia.

LinkedIn allows users to connect with each other through 'gated access'. You've got to know someone who knows someone. If you invite too many people who label an invite 'I don't know' or 'spam', you will be given a warning or have your account suspended or closed. So send an introductory message when you are linking in with someone you may have met at a cocktail party, to jog their memory about the connection. A tiered contact network of first-, second- and third-degree connections is familiar—you can ask someone you know to introduce you to someone you would like to know, as in the past.

Social HR

Employers use LinkedIn to list jobs and search for potential candidates. They also use LinkedIn Company Pages to showcase their companies.

Social media is playing an increasingly important role in HR, so much so that 'Social HR' is now a recognisable term. Recruiting firms like Entelo, Gild, TalentBin, the UK's thesocialCV and Australia's Firebrand Talent are using big social data to find talent.

Author of *The 2020 Workplace* Jeanne Meister says social media is critical for finding top talent and for most Millennials, as a survey by Spherion Staffing shows, an employer's online reputation matters as much as the job it offers. Millennial employees, who will make up 50 per cent of the 2020 workplace, believe technology is indispensable to creating value at work. But it's not just about Millennials; as we saw earlier, with some variance the greatest growth on social platforms is among those aged 45 and above.

'According to a Microsoft survey,' Meister says, 'of 9000 workers across 32 countries, 31 per cent would be willing to spend their own money on a new social tool if it made them more efficient at work.'

Recruiters are engaging with big data, analysing candidates' social media profiles but also their activity on specialty sites specific to their professions, such as the open-source community forums Stack Overflow and GitHub (for coders), Proformative (for accountants) and Dribbble (for designers). The algorithms they use give them the heads-up on candidates who are readying themselves to enter the job market (a bio update, for example), allowing them to locate key talent before competitors.

Professionals can also use LinkedIn groups to connect with others in moderated groups where links to information can be shared and discussed.

Most people use the free versions of LinkedIn although I use the premium, paid version.

People use LinkedIn to:

- research people and companies (75.8 per cent)
- reconnect with colleagues (70.6 per cent)
- build new relationships (45 per cent)
- increase the effectiveness of face-to-face networking (41.2 per cent).

LinkedIn recently reported that high net wealth professionals are increasingly using it to help them make financial decisions. Whether or not investors have advisers, they are actively using social media research to inform investment decisions. LinkedIn is considered an invaluable asset for the ultra-affluent.

Case studies

LinkedIn showcases a number of successful case studies on its website. For example, it shows how sponsored links can increase the reach of content, particularly valuable to brands seeking to reach high net wealth professionals. Mercedes-Benz US used this approach to increase visibility of the new E and S class models, and was able to adapt its campaign execution as real-time analytics provided information on audience responses.

When I left my role as an executive to start up my social media consultancy I announced the change on my LinkedIn profile. Within a few minutes (literally) I was contacted by someone who had been following my updates and commentary. He later became a client.

Here are some other ways executives are using it:

- *To learn about people before you meet them.* Here you have to strike the right balance between interest and stalking. But it's no different from how we would turn up to a job interview having thoroughly researched a company. Showing a genuine interest in people is critical to forming good relationships. It's also a conversation starter. If someone has worked in South Africa and you were born there, it's a perfect opening. The key here is to be open and authentic in how you respond to what you've learned. I recently met with a prospect in a financial services firm to talk about training the executive team in social media. I mentioned that I'd read her LinkedIn profile and seen she'd had long stints overseas, including in London. As I have a sister there and often travel to the UK, we could talk about some favourite places. I let people know if I've read their profile because it's more open to do so.

- *To generate business.* There are countless case studies of people using LinkedIn to generate business. James Filbird is often mentioned because he used LinkedIn almost exclusively to build his business. He owns JMF International Trade Group Ltd, a company he built to $5 million in revenue. He focused on LinkedIn because, among other things, the platform is accessible within China. (Many others are blocked, although there are Chinese equivalents.) He built out his profile, joined the maximum allowable 50 groups and spent up to two hours daily on the site engaging in group discussions so he could get introduced to and maintain relationships with like-minded individuals. Filbird says 75 per cent of his business comes from LinkedIn. Using LinkedIn to develop his network has consistently led to new business opportunities for his American-owned, China-based consulting firm.

- *To find jobs.* Singling out a success story here seems silly because finding jobs through LinkedIn is par for the course. Companies increasingly post job ads on the site, but the networking opportunities also lead to meetings and offers.

- *To position your expertise and stand out.* Recruiters are constantly trawling LinkedIn profiles looking for those out-of-the-box talents who network professionally, and curate and share valuable content. Also, recruiters looking for people based on keyword searches can match you to a role you're actually passionate about.

- *For precision marketing.* Kyle Lacy has shared good case studies on how LinkedIn can be used for precision marketing and sales. One is of Peter Taliangis, a real estate agent who used LinkedIn to sell a $300 000 home in Western Australia after being approached on LinkedIn by a prospective buyer. The deal was closed before the official 'open for inspection' event took place.

Social issues

Like all social media networks, LinkedIn is balancing the need to give users integration while managing their privacy, being open and yet secure.

LinkedIn has come under criticism for Intro, an app that allows LinkedIn to intercept email and shows how you are connected to people. Security experts say this is a big no-no. TechCrunch's Matthew Panzarino, for example, argues that handing over email access to a third party is a security risk but could also be against IT policies. He advises that corporate clients with sensitive email should never allow it to be transmitted via a proxy.

LinkedIn has also experienced password losses and is implicated in a class action regarding email.

Me 3.0

In an age of algorithms, who you are is in part determined by your digital footprint, which means that if you network for business then you will need to do so online.

While business is in some ways the same as it ever was (based on mutually beneficial relationships), social media has turned the way we form those relationships on its head. No matter how well you're doing with your current communication, you need to look ahead and adapt the way you connect and communicate to keep up with this change.

Naturally how you use the platform depends on what you want to achieve, and that will vary widely. You can use it for raising funds, recruitment, job search or networking with peers, among other things.

Let's go—LinkedIn

Go to the LinkedIn.com registration page and sign up (figure 10.1).

Figure 10.1: signing up with LinkedIn

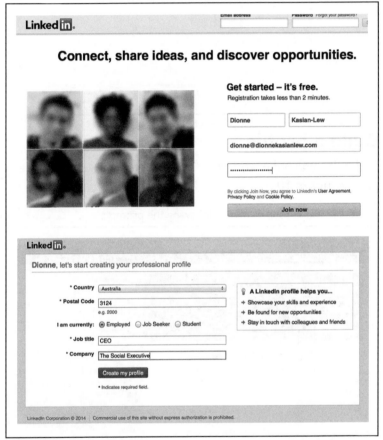

LinkedIn will ask you if you want it to access your email contacts. I skip this step. After confirming your email with the network, you will then be able to build your platform (figure 10.2, overleaf).

Figure 10.2: adding your email

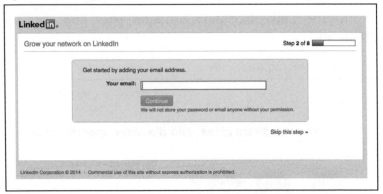

Build a profile

LinkedIn will take you step by step through establishing a profile (figure 10.3).

Figure 10.3: build your profile by following the prompts

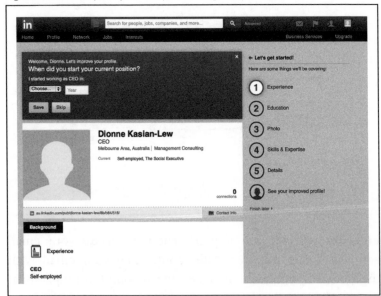

When prompted to add a photo, simply click the upload button, adjust the photograph and save (figure 10.4).

Figure 10.4: make sure you include a recent, professional photo

I am often asked whether professionals should use photos. I know that in pre-social days some recruiters thought it bad taste to send a photo, but in the digital era it's important to bring a human element to your online profiles.

Use a recent, high-quality close-up photograph. People like to deal with people. Remember too that digital does not replace real-life connection—it extends it. Many virtual connections become a part of real life and this creates continuity. Faceless avatars are off-putting, and on some social media platforms like

Twitter the 'bots' that clean up fake accounts classify them as spam. When you first develop a profile you'll see at bottom left that your LinkedIn address, which is the link you will send to others to help them find your profile, shows a random jumble of letters after your name (figure 10.5). This is unprofessional. It's simple to customise. Make sure you do so right away as they are first come, first served.

Figure 10.5: complex LinkedIn URL with numbers and letters after name

Move your cursor over Profile at the top of your Home page and select Edit Profile (figure 10.6).

Figure 10.6: LinkedIn's Edit Profile

Click Edit next to the URL under your profile photo. It will open up a new page (figure 10.7).

Figure 10.7: customising your public URL

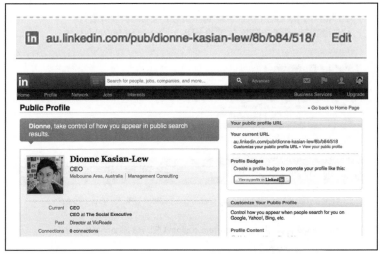

If you look on the right you'll see your public profile. Click 'Customize your public profile URL'. Type the last part of your new custom URL in the text box. If the name is available, a green tick will appear. Click the Set Custom URL button and you're done (figure 10.8, overleaf).

Figure 10.8: click the 'Customize your public profile' URL link

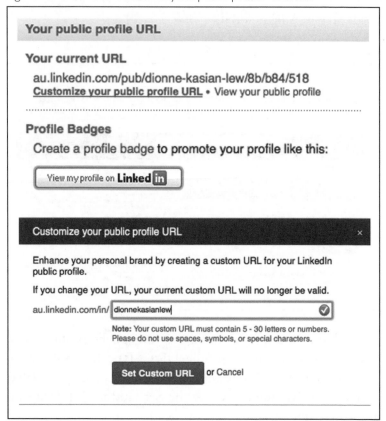

LinkedIn things to remember

- Your custom URL must have between 5 and 30 letters or numbers with no spaces, symbols or special characters.

- You cannot change your URL more than three times in six months.

- URLs aren't available on request so if you can't find what you want, choose the next best thing.

Use your LinkedIn URL to build influence

Now that you have a LinkedIn address, you can add it to other social media sites, such as Twitter, or as part of your email signature.

You can also add a View My LinkedIn Profile button to a blog or online résumé. If you want to do so, head to www .linkedin.com/profile/profile-badges and follow the prompts (figure 10.9).

Figure 10.9: adding a LinkedIn button

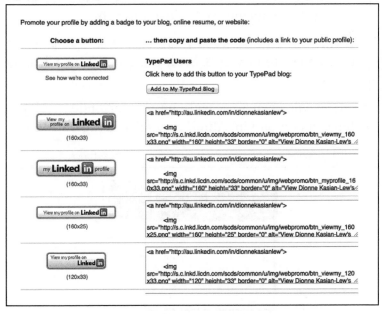

Finesse your profile

You can finesse your profile by making changes in the Edit Profile menu.

Remember that unless you choose to switch off your broadcast options, every time you make a change to your profile it will let all your contacts know. Many a LinkedIn user has received a flood of congratulations for a new role when all they've done is to change a few words in their profile description.

Switching broadcasts off allows you to tinker to your heart's content. If, however, you do switch roles or you want to send signals to recruiters that you're updating your bio in preparation for a move, then remember to switch it back on.

To switch off broadcasts, go to your Account & Settings at top right then down to Privacy & Settings (figure 10.10). Click on this option.

The page will open to a wide number of options. Almost anything you do on LinkedIn is customisable (figure 10.11).

Figure 10.10: switching off broadcast — under privacy settings

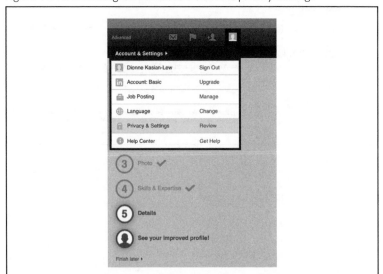

Figure 10.11: switching off broadcast—under privacy controls

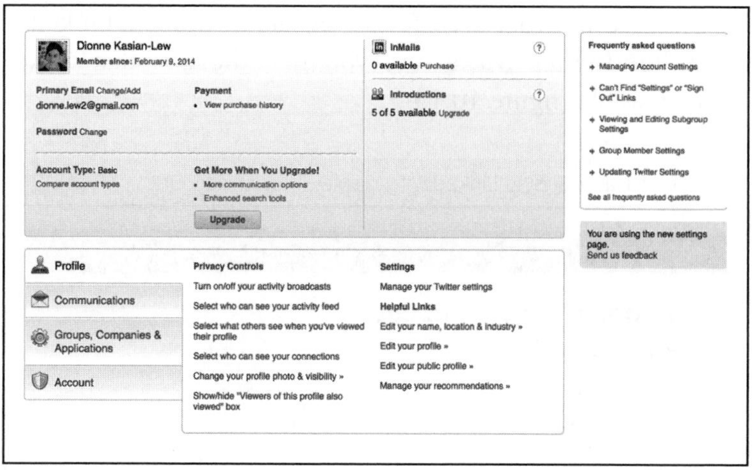

The first option under Privacy Controls allows you to turn on/off your activity broadcasts. Open and make sure you untick this box (figure 10.12).

Figure 10.12: untick box to switch off activity broadcast

While we're here, you'll see under Settings that you can add your Twitter link. Do so. This will allow you to push something from Twitter directly into LinkedIn by adding the hashtag #li or #in at the end of your tweet.

LinkedIn will need you to authorise the app to access Twitter. Do so. You can revoke access to an app at any time on LinkedIn or within Twitter. Make sure you tick the box that makes Twitter visible (figure 10.13).

Figure 10.13: authorising LinkedIn to display Twitter account

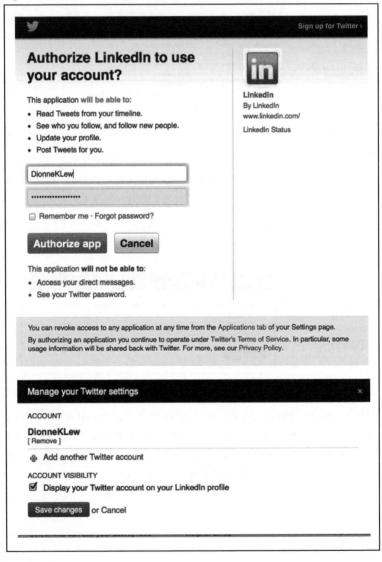

Your headline

Your 120–character headline is prime real estate so use it to differentiate yourself (figure 10.14). There are lots of 'senior executives' out there. Be the 'not-for-profit CEO who successfully delivered a 500 per cent increase in diabetes funding in two years'. The key words in your headline affect how you will be found, so ensure they're in your title. You can put your current job title, but think how many CEOs there are in a 200 million–strong pool. Say something about yourself.

Figure 10.14: use your 120-character headline to differentiate yourself

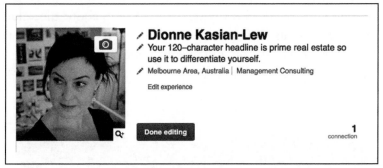

Your employment history

Your employment history provides legitimacy, particularly if it comes with credible recommendations. You don't need to write *War and Peace* though.

Who should I connect with?

You need to build strategic connections with influencers, colleagues and potential business interests.

But algorithms also work out your interests and throw unknowns in your path. How open you are to them depends on your personality. Only connecting if there's a potential business outcome feels to me a bit like pyramid selling. I've met up with many people just because I found them interesting. It's enriching and I've made many amazing contacts as a result.

Recommendations and endorsements

LinkedIn allows you to ask for or make recommendations.

Do you have to reciprocate when someone recommends you? The answer is no—as in real life, so online. Your recommendations go to your reputation so use them judiciously. But where they are deserved, go ahead.

LinkedIn also prompts you to endorse the skills of people you are connected with (figure 10.15). Views about the value of endorsements differ. Only endorse people for skills you *know* they have. If you mistakenly endorse someone, don't worry—you can withdraw it.

Figure 10.15: LinkedIn makes endorsement suggestions

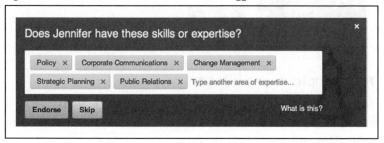

In many countries, displaying false endorsements or testimonials could be deceptive conduct. In Australia, for example, Jamie White, Director of Pod Legal, says:

> Accepting and displaying endorsements and testimonials on your LinkedIn page may be a great vote for your credentials. However, allowing inflated, false or inaccurate feedback to be published on your LinkedIn page (or other social media pages) could lead to legal action and fines.

Be sure you know the law in your country.

What do I share?

You can share content from most sites by pressing the LinkedIn share button (figure 10.16). The content will automatically show up in your stream and anyone in your network can see it. Comment on articles you find interesting.

Figure 10.16: share publicly from the 'Share an update' space

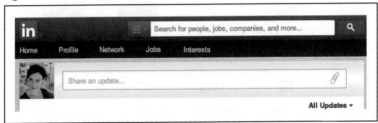

If you type in the full name of a person in the text, LinkedIn will prompt them that they've been mentioned, which creates a conversation. You can also use the 'share an update' space on your Home page to send updates or information. There's a lot of good content on LinkedIn running through this page that you can read and share from within the site.

What are groups and should I join them?

LinkedIn will recommend some groups for you to follow when you first join up (figure 10.17, overleaf). This is a great way to start making connections. Simply join a group and you can then share posts and engage in discussions with other users.

Figure 10.17: joining LinkedIn groups is easy

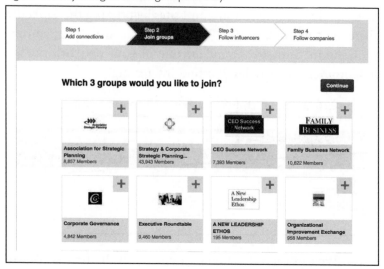

Groups bring together people with strong interests and can be great for exchanging views. Some people, however, just post links to their own content and don't add to the community. As a result, the value varies greatly.

If you are time poor, which most executives are, I'd try niche groups with members who are seriously interested in a topic. Some of the biggest 'brand' groups generate lots of thumbs up and 'love it' comments, which are quite exhausting to scroll through.

A huge benefit of groups is that they allow you to connect through your LinkedIn email with people who are not in your tiered contact network. This is important. You are going to encounter experts with whom you want to connect; groups will give you the opportunity to take the relationship further.

Where possible, and when the time is right, it's good to connect with people in real life. All the usual caveats around online safety apply.

Who is checking me out?

You can change the way you appear on LinkedIn in Privacy and Settings by clicking on 'What others see when you've viewed their profile' (figure 10.18).

Figure 10.18: manage what others see when you view their profile

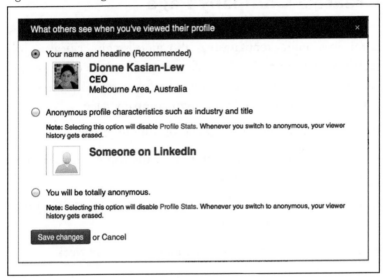

Some people prefer to remain anonymous (figure 10.19).

Figure 10.19: an anonymous member views your profile

Some people find this confronting and even 'stalky'. It does have its uses though, for example if you are researching job candidates and want to keep your search private. Many recruiters use it in this way. Personally, I don't like it but it comes with the platform, at least at this stage.

I tend to show my full details because I want people to know I've taken the time and effort to read their profile and understand their needs; and as I've said, I will be sure to drop this into conversation.

Create a Company Page

It goes without staying that this is important for brands. A company's online reputation is also increasingly critical to job seekers who value technologically savvy and engaged companies. As someone who is using LinkedIn for personal professional reasons, you do not need your own company page.

If you're a small business you can set one up easily.

- Move your cursor over Interests at the top of your Home page and select Companies.

- Click the Create link in the Create a Company Page box on the right of the page.

- Enter your company's official name and your work email address.

- Click Continue and enter your company information. In order to publish your Company Page you must include a company description and website URL.

SlideShare

As a professional, it's important to showcase professional expertise, including through your presentations.

We will set up SlideShare in the next chapter, but remember to embed your presentations in your LinkedIn Home page.

You can do this by editing your Background and adding a link or uploading a file directly (figure 10.20). You can upload a file straight from the desktop.

Figure 10.20: adding SlideShare links

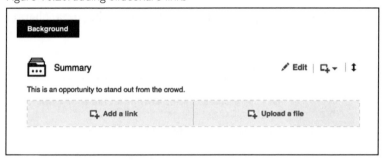

Or you can Add a link using the URL that SlideShare gives you when you create a presentation—just remember to click the Add Link button at the bottom when you're done (figure 10.21).

Figure 10.21: adding a link

You can share directly from SlideShare by choosing the Post to LinkedIn option, as we will see in the next chapter (figure 10.22).

Figure 10.22: adding a link from SlideShare

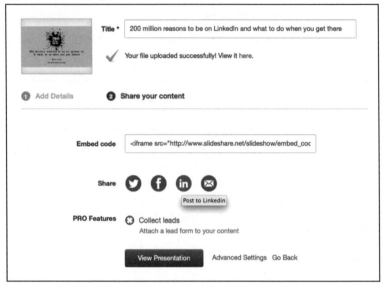

Can I outsource my LinkedIn engagement?

Would you send your assistant to a cocktail party to speak on your behalf? I don't think so. Why is LinkedIn different? A virtual connection is a personal connection that has not yet made its way into real life. By all means get a consultant to set up, brand or teach you LinkedIn. But engagement is about the real you.

This chapter will get you up and running on LinkedIn, but once you've learned the ropes you may want to amp it up with some bootcamp suggestions. These are pro tips. I've included sources for these great tips so you can look up authorities and follow their other fabulous suggestions.

LinkedIn bootcamp

- Think about the keywords people would use to find you (not your job title) when you fill out your profile. (Jill Duffy, *PC Mag*)

- To generate a quick résumé based on your LinkedIn profile, give LinkedIn's Resume Builder a try. (Kristin Burnham, *Information Week*)

- LinkedIn applications allow you to enhance your profile in different ways: bloggers can add the WordPress app that synchs with a blog: the Box.net app enables you to embed videos. (Brian Voo, Hongkiat)

- Segment your connections by tagging them so you can send personalised communications. (Joshua Steimle, *Forbes*)

- Do a profile-by-profile review of your direct connections. You can remove connections that don't add value — they are not notified when they're removed. (JD Gershbein, *Huffington Post*)

Chapter summary

Use LinkedIn to make mutually beneficial connections, share expertise, follow companies and search for talent. More than 250 million professionals from over 200 countries are in this professional networking hub. LinkedIn allows unprecedented and borderless collaboration, and allows you to bring digital connections into real life.

CHAPTER 11

SlideShare: it's a pump class for PowerPoint

As in real life, so online. You used to deliver a PowerPoint presentation to a defined audience at a single moment in time, photocopying or sharing the content first via email then by passing on a USB stick to those who could not be there. Now you use SlideShare to reach a global audience by sharing rich presentations that can be stored online, shared with a link and viewed at any time.

A SlideShare snapshot

It's	a social network for slides
	YouTube for PowerPoint
Started	March 2006
Current number of users	200 million
Important because	it's familiar, relevant to your audience
Worrying because	not enough people know about it

Socialised PowerPoint

Think of professional information sessions and you'd be hard pressed not to think of PowerPoint or other such tools that use film, photographs, charts—and, sadly, far too many dot points—to communicate.

Whether at a boardroom meeting or a conference drawing thousands, communicators like to use different tools to make a point and audiences like to receive information in multiple formats. This is familiar territory.

In the past, presentations were limited by time, space and audience. You had to be there to see the presentation. You had to remember what was said. If you were lucky the presenter photocopied it onto A4 sheets with little boxes and notes so you could refer to talking points and share it with others you thought would benefit from the message.

SlideShare builds on this—only it's better, because it allows you to share your work with a global audience and view the work of others who are sharing within it.

SlideShare was launched in October 2006 as a YouTube for slide presentations. Although there are alternatives, such as Scribd.com, Issuu and Docstoc, right now SlideShare is the best known such platform. I prefer to think of it as a socialised PowerPoint because I associate YouTube with downloading videos. You can share any type of digital content on SlideShare, including documents, infographics, webcasts and video. It can be viewed from the site, on mobile or embedded elsewhere, such as on the Home page of your intranet or a blog. And with 60 million monthly visitors and 130 million page views, it's one of the top 200 sites on the internet and a great place to be heard.

It takes the same amount of hard work to prepare a good slide presentation whether it's viewed by five people or 15 000.

Think of all the knowledge contained in traditional presentations made around the world but how little was available to you unless you were lucky enough to see it. SlideShare allows people to rate, comment on and share the uploaded content. You can learn a lot in this process. For example, you could put up a graph of the latest social media use data and have someone point you to revisions or updated statistics. The added ability to comment means you can open up a dialogue with experts in your field, or just people interested in a topic, that enhances your understanding.

And the information you post is searchable not just within SlideShare but from within search engines such as Google.

Here are some of SlideShare's advantages:

- Presentations are tagged with key words, making them searchable.

- You can find presentations from experts around the world.

- You choose what you want to view and when you want to view it.

- You can share your expertise.

- You can embed the information into a blog post (provided you properly acknowledge the source) to illustrate a point or share statistics.

- You can share the presentation on other social media sites and blogs, using them as links to the presentation where you have all the time and space in the world to express your view as you would wish.

- You don't need to email or use a USB to share the files—you simply point people to a web address, which is permanent.

SlideShare was originally meant for businesses to share slides among employees more easily, but like most social media networks it has evolved in response to the way it is used. Not only do people use it to showcase personal views or company information, but many presentations are uploaded for entertainment value. Although it's primarily for sharing slides it also supports documents, PDFs, videos and webinars, and was voted among the world's top 10 tools for education and e-learning in 2010.

You can also broadcast a video or audio conference through SlideShare using its Zipcast feature. Users can communicate during the presentation via an inbuilt chat function, as in an interactive classroom. Paid services such as WebEx and GoToMeeting have similar capability and allow you to share your computer screen with users.

SlideShare was acquired last year by LinkedIn, which means you can now embed presentations into your LinkedIn profile. This allows you to showcase your work or that of your company, and you can use it to direct people to LinkedIn Company Pages or your website.

Most of SlideShare's audience is made up of business people actively looking for information about one topic or another, so if you have something to say on a subject you already have a captive audience.

The average SlideShare reader will give you eight minutes of their time and view 20 slides — that's a lot of attention in our highly distracted world.

And it's a site that's about business. The six most-used tags on SlideShare are:

- business
- market
- trends
- research

- social media

- statistics.

But there is no reason this should be limited and every indication that as more people hop on board, it will shift.

Case studies

In the case study section the company lists numerous examples of how SlideShare can be used to increase your professional and business reach, whether you're an entrepreneur, a thought leader, or a B2B or B2C company.

One example profiled by SlideShare relates how startup Framebench used it to attract customer leads. The CEO, Rohit Agarwal, used SlideShare as part of a social media mix and a content distribution channel to deliver his content to nearly 60 million professionals.

Initially, Framebench converted an existing blog post into a presentation and got 8000 views. This was enough to convince the business that the platform was right for their needs. Second time around they purposely designed a presentation with great visuals and short, punchy messages. It received 400000 views in just two weeks. From a business perspective, this is why those views were important:

- The high visibility led to increased website traffic and 500 sign-ups for the product in just three days.

- It generated 75 leads for Framebench, 20 per cent of which were qualified, and about 5 per cent of which were active users. Of the 500 sign-ups, 45 per cent are currently active users of the product.

For executives, SlideShare is a great place for thought leadership because you're not limited in length and you can associate the presentation with your professional profile. The URL to your SlideShare is permanent, which means you can add it to your email signature, and refer to it within presentations or pitches—in other words, use it in any way that's aligned with your business strategy.

Social issues

As with any content you produce, make sure you have all the right attributions; in particular, because this is a visual platform, make sure you are using photographic licences correctly.

10 sites that offer great free visuals (courtesy of Dustin Senos, on Medium):

1   Little Visuals (http://littlevisuals.co/)

2   Unsplash (http://unsplash.com/)

3   Death to the Stock Photo (http://join.deathtothestockphoto.com/)

4   New Old Stock (http://nos.twnsnd.co/)

5   Superfamous (requires attribution) (http://superfamous.com/)

6   Picjumbo (http://picjumbo.com/)

7   The Pattern Library (http://thepatternlibrary.com/)

8   Gratisography (http://www.gratisography.com/)

9   Getrefe (http://getrefe.tumblr.com/)

10 IM Free (requires attribution) (http://imcreator.com/free)

Me 3.0

Should you be using SlideShare? Yes, it fits perfectly with an executive platform. It's social media for professionals. The fact that your presentations can be showcased on your LinkedIn page really goes to the issue of credibility: you demonstrate through content that professionally you can put your money where your mouth is.

As on all social media platforms you need to tailor your content for the medium. Twitter, for example, requires 140-character bursts of text that lead people to great content through links or add value through comments.

On SlideShare there are no limits—either on length or on the sorts of materials you can include. As a guide, brand specialist David Brier says 45 per cent of SlideShares have 10–30 slides, with an average of 24 words per slide. Although it's good to have guides, my personal belief is that content should be as long or as short as it needs to be. Some stories take a long time to tell, others don't. A good narrator will use the right amount of material needed for maximum impact.

Some general tips on presentation content

- You can't use the same presentation you gave to your team if you had to be there to add in missing information. Think like the person who is going to read it. What would you need to see to get the complete picture?

- Before you publish anything, work out your story—what you have to say and how you are going to say it.

- Add keywords to the title, description and tags.

- Start with the big picture and drill down to the detail.

- Cover one message per slide.

- A picture paints a thousand words (but remember, because you're not presenting it personally it has to make sense in isolation).

- As ever, design your presentation.

- Promote it.

- Include a call to action on the last slide.

- Capture the details of people who respond. Add them to a Twitter list or read their material—there's a reason you're resonating with each other.

Let's go—SlideShare

Go to Slideshare.net and sign up (figure 11.1). I have a premium account because it allows me to upload large presentations and gives me the option of sharing with anyone or with limited groups, although I've never used the latter. Sign in using either your LinkedIn or your Facebook account. I use LinkedIn because I also embed my presentations into my LinkedIn profile.

Figure 11.1: the SlideShare Home page

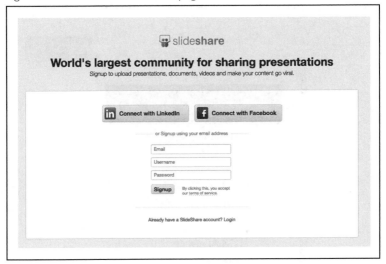

Tick the boxes that allow SlideShare and LinkedIn to connect and Save Settings, then go set up your account (figure 11.2, overleaf).

Figure 11.2: setting up SlideShare

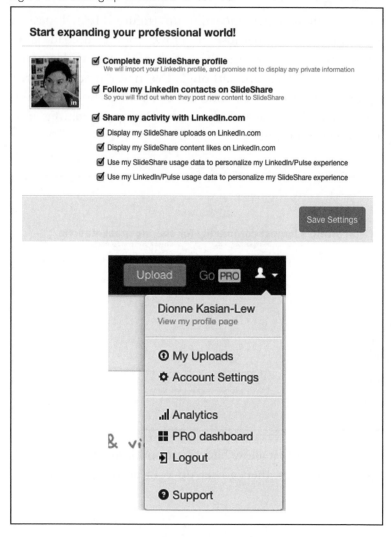

You'll see that SlideShare offers analytics. The PRO version allows you to manage leads and is good for marketers but not essential for an individual professional platform. You can manage sharing, email, privacy and content from Account Settings. Connect up your social media networks under Sharing (figure 11.3).

Figure 11.3: set up your profile under General

Getting started

SlideShare will provide some popular presentations for you to view.

To upload a presentation use the orange button if you're on the free version or the blue button if you're on premium and want to share videos to private groups (figure 11.4).

Figure 11.4: upload buttons

Follow the prompts and make sure you give your presentation an interesting description that people will want to read.

You can upload a PowerPoint directly but sometimes the design can go out of kilter, so I always save mine as a PDF first. You can do this by going to 'Print your PowerPoint', where you are offered this option (figure 11.5).

Figure 11.5: saving PowerPoint as a PDF

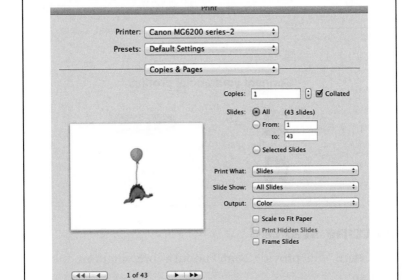

You can then use the social share buttons to push the presentation out through your various networks. Make sure you post it to your LinkedIn account using the IN button (figure 11.6).

Figure 11.6: share to LinkedIn account using button

You can view your presentation from your Home page. LinkedIn will learn about your preferences from the way you tag content, and make suggestions on the right. You'll be able to see how many views your presentation gets, and to view and respond to comments (figure 11.7).

Figure 11.7: viewing your presentation

Grow your network

There are many presentations on the SlideShare network itself that will help you learn how to grow your reputation and influence, such as this one by Jeff Bullas (figure 11.8).

Figure 11.8: Jeff Bullas's SlideShare account

This chapter will get you up and running on SlideShare, but once you've learned the ropes you may want to amp it up with some bootcamp suggestions. These are pro tips. I've included sources for these great tips so you can look up authorities and follow their other fabulous suggestions.

SlideShare bootcamp

- Use one large visual metaphor per slide and 1–3 sentences of advice on the image maximum. (Kristina Allen)

- Get maximum mileage out of your SlideShare by making it the basis for links to other content such as images, blogs and ebooks. (Miranda Miller)

- Use Font Squirrel to pick beautiful fonts and Compfight to find stunning Creative Commons images. (Kissmetrics)

- Combine SlideShare with Pinterest—Pinterest is a pinboard-style photo sharing website http://about .pinterest.com/. (Sharon Hurley Hall)

Chapter summary

It takes the same amount of hard work to prepare a good slide presentation whether it's viewed by five people or 15000, in a room or around the world. SlideShare allows you to share your work with a global audience and view the work of others who are sharing within it. With 60 million monthly visitors and 130 million page views, it's one of the top 200 sites on the internet and a great place to be heard.

CHAPTER 12

Google Plus: your social rolodex

As in real life, so online. You used to link up with colleagues and family, get involved in groups with shared interests and meet up to connect. You can do all those things on Google Plus, plus...you can share posts, chat, hangout in video, jump in on hangouts that experts you don't know are having across the world (permission interrupting), set up events, and go local by connecting with people and businesses around you. Google Plus is a social rolodex, only it also creates the social layer it categorises.

A Google Plus snapshot

It's	a social layer
Started	2011
Current user numbers	200 million
Important because	it's an integrated ecosystem
Worrying because	it's harder to learn

What would you call a place where people you knew were neatly categorised into circles that allowed you to share information with them either discretely or simultaneously through a broad public broadcast? Where you could hang out with an individual or group at a moment's notice or by clicking on a button from your Google calendar? Where could you drop into a videocast just because of its title, hear experts sharing, or create a place for like-minded communities to share information and talk.

It's hard to think of a real-life equivalent, but that's Google Plus. Social rolodex meets augmented reality, except it's real.

The backstory

Google Plus was added to Google in 2011 to compete with Facebook, which has over a billion users. It currently has 540 million active users, not bad when you consider it's a little over two years old while Facebook is about to celebrate its tenth birthday.

Google Plus is a social layer rather than a social network because it adds that connectivity to pretty much anything you do in the Google ecosystem. And that's huge if you think that Google is about:

- Search
- Maps
- YouTube
- Gmail
- Android
- Google Play
- Google Music
- Google Voice
- Google Wallet
- Google Local

... and much more.

Remember, Google aims to organise the world's information — and you are a part of that world.

Important issues

If producing quality content is part of your personal brand then you need to establish your authority as a writer on Google by setting up Google Authorship. This boosts your status on Google and also increases the likelihood of your content being found through search.

We talked earlier in the book about how people find you on Google. Although the algorithm keeps changing, everything you do on Google Plus is indexed and so counts towards making you more visible.

Case studies

London-based reporter Sean O'Neill recently wrote a great case study of how UK online travel agency Travel Republic attracted over a million followers on Google in a year, helping it to reach its goal of engaging with existing and potential customers beyond the UK (figure 12.1). The brand now has well over two million followers.

Figure 12.1: Travel Republic Google Plus page

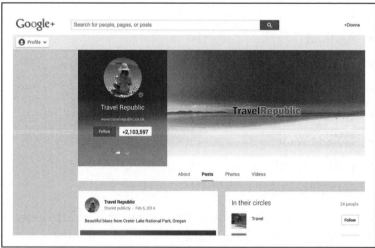

The agency posted mainly visual content with great results. Traffic to some hotels went up by as much as 633 per cent following a Google Plus post.

In October 2012, a Travel Republic post on the Ubud Hanging Gardens in Bali received 3231 +1's and its link to TravelRepublic.com received 7450 clicks. These were some of the Google Plus strategies that were used:

- It was promoted on Google Plus via What's Hot— that's random.

- It set up Google Plus communities such as Beach Holidays.

- Travel Republic installed the Google+ badge on its Home page, displaying the number of followers and encouraging others to join its page.

- It added a +1 button to email marketing.

Me 3.0

Google Plus is a bit more technical than other platforms, but for those who are serious about personal branding and influence it can't be ignored.

As I've said, authorship combined with posts that are shared in Google Plus ensure you are visible and authoritative. Google Plus also allows you to see who has shared your content through Google+ Ripples, a good way to identify potential fans and focus your energy on building key relationships.

You can also personalise your search results from Google Plus by switching on personalised search. This shows you who shared your content as well as those to whom they are connected, giving you the chance to build a fan base.

Let's go—Google Plus

Set up a Google or Gmail account. I won't guide you through that as it's something you'll be familiar with. Once you have a Google account, upgrade it to Google Plus (figure 12.2).

Figure 12.2: upgrade to Google Plus

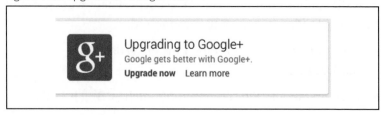

You can reach your Google Plus from the menu in the top right of your screen, which shows your name with a + sign next to it (figure 12.3).

Figure 12.3: moving from Gmail to Google Plus means moving from a private to a public world

Before you push this button, you're in your Google or Gmail but in the private world. Once you push this button, you go into the social layer, which is a public network. I can't stress this enough because the move into Google Plus is so seamless that you can forget you've changed locations.

The Google Plus landscape

Figure 12.4 shows what it will look like when you enter the Google Plus environment.

Figure 12.4: the Google Plus environment

On the right you'll see that you can go back to your private email at any time by clicking on your photo.

The square icon unlocks the door to the Google ecosystem (figure 12.5).

Figure 12.5: Google apps

So many parts of your life are represented here, including your contacts, calendars, groups and mail. If you push the More button, Google shows you other things you can do in its ecosystem (figure 12.6).

Figure 12.6: more Google apps

Many people don't know there's a translation service directly available to you on email. It's imperfect, but helpful. Likewise, because Google owns YouTube you can go straight to your personal channel from here.

You can set up a blog using Blogger or use other alternatives outside of Google, like WordPress. Click 'Even more from Google' and a whole universe opens up (figure 12.7).

Figure 12.7: more options open up as you click into the menu

Google Keep is a bookmarking platform, like Evernote.

You can set up Alerts for any key words here. As a professional you should set up alerts for your name and business name so you are alerted if something happens online that mentions you. Simply click on the Alert button and fill out the window that pops up (figure 12.8).

Figure 12.8: setting up a Google alert

All the things you can do on Google Plus are hidden under the Home button on the left (figure 12.9).

Figure 12.9: Home on Google Plus

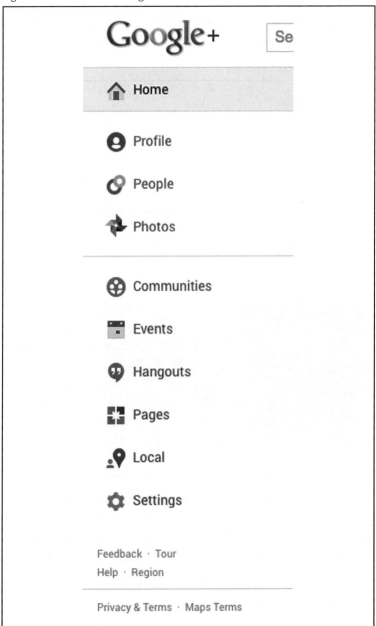

Creating a profile

The first thing you need to do is to create your profile. Click on the profile button then select a profile photo (figure 12.10).

Figure 12.10: upload a photo

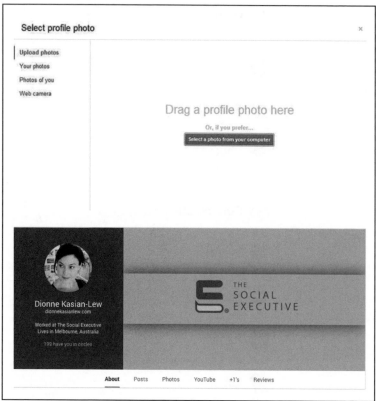

Make sure it's similar to other photos of you on social media networks so you create a recognisable personal brand. If you are a personal brand then add a business identity as well, although you can create a separate Google Plus page for business.

On your profile page, you'll find a bar with the buttons About, Posts, Photos, YouTube, +1s and Reviews:

- *About.* Here's where you introduce yourself and indicate your interests (figure 12.11).

Figure 12.11: fill out the About section

Story

Tagline
CEO | Author | Professional Speaker | Strategist | Blogger

Introduction

As a 'multi-hyphenate' I have two profiles on Google+.

This one is predominantly for my role as CEO of The Social Executive™ a leadership consultancy training Boards, C-Suites and professionals on how to use social and digital media for business.

I am a published author of The Social Executive (Dugdale-Woolf Publishing) and Relevance! and a contributor to to Leading Company, Smart Company and Company Director. I am a professional speaker represented by ICMI, a strategist and member of the Australian Institute of Company Directors.

I blog at The Connected Leader on leadership including the challenges of leading in the digital era.

I also blog at Be Your Whole Self where I synthesize insights from psychology, philosophy, art to publish insights on how to be your whole, complex, contradictory, beautiful self. The Be Your Whole Self: where self-help fails book is now available.

I am a lover of art, design, science, philosophy, psychology; executive by day and writer/painter by day and night.

Bragging rights
Examples: survived high school, have 3 kids, etc.

- *Posts.* To write a post click Home at top left and then 'Share what's new ...' (figure 12.12, overleaf). There's no word limit and you can add photos, videos or links. You can share it with circles or publicly, or both.

Figure 12.12: share what's new

- *Photos.* All photos added here are public.

- *YouTube.* You can set up your YouTube channel from within Google Plus. This is vital for many businesses. It's also important when building a personal platform, but many executives with a full-time role feel it's a bridge too far. We're not going to head down that path, although I mention it now because the growth and popularity of video cannot be ignored. If you want to explore simply click on the YouTube button and follow the prompts to set up your channel (figure 12.13).

- *+1.* If you like a post and want to share it, click the +1 button. Anything you've shared in this way will appear in the +1 section of your profile. These contribute to your platform and influence search.

Figure 12.13: access YouTube through Google Plus

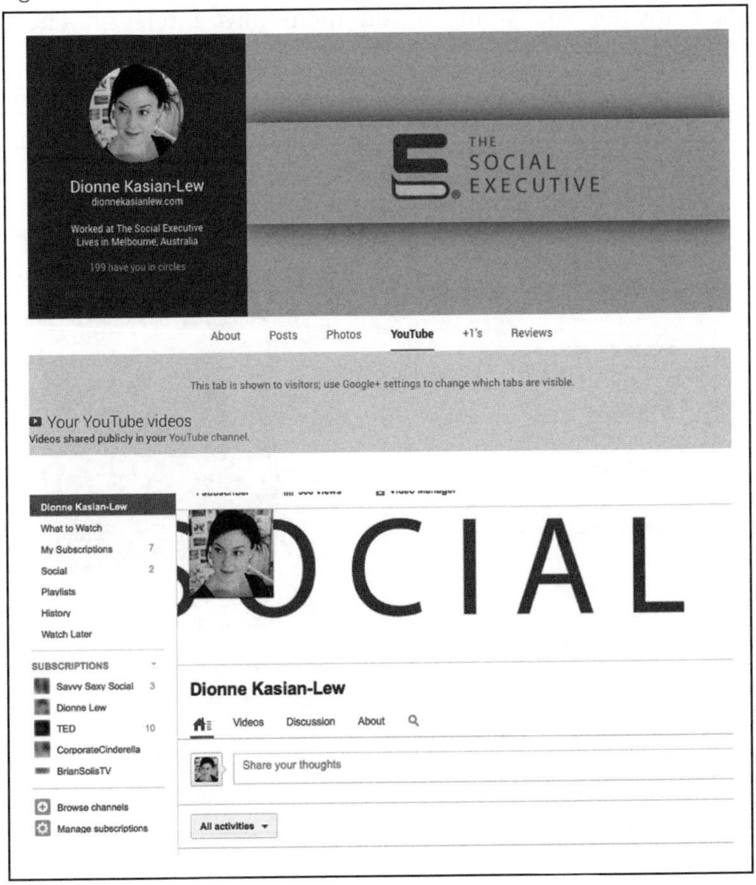

People

You'll find people to follow under People. No surprises there. In this section you can create Circles, which are your social rolodex. They allow you to categorise under, say, Family, Suppliers, Recruitment Prospects—whatever you want. Only you will know how you've identified them. If you are developing country-based networks you might group people by Australia, Bermuda, Canada and so forth.

When you open People, Google will also make suggestions—click anyone you want to add them into a relevant circle (figure 12.14).

Figure 12.14: adding people to circles

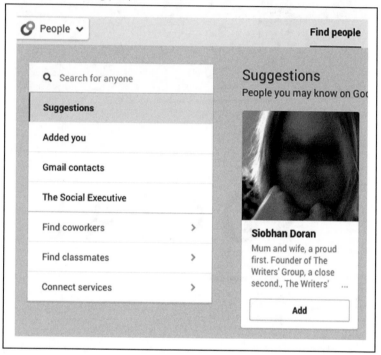

Like Twitter, and unlike Facebook, Google Plus allows for one-sided following. When you add someone to your circles, they don't have to add you back.

Communities

Communities on Google Plus are highly engaged and can be found under the Communities section (figure 12.15).

Figure 12.15: Google+ Communities

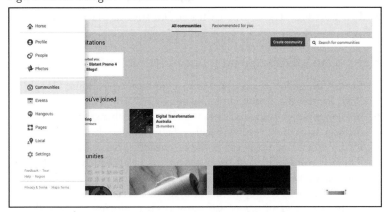

Google Plus provides active communities who come together around a certain topic, such as leadership. For example, I am part of the #leadwithgiants community (figure 12.16).

Figure 12.16: the Lead With Giants leadership community

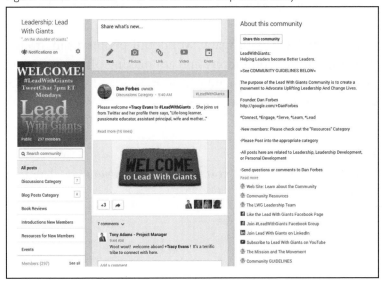

The group comes together to share blog posts and discussion, and to connect across our other social media platforms as well. These communities are highly engaged.

Here's Dan V. Forbes, who founded #Leadwithgiants:

> Lead With Giants is a Social Media Community spanning Google Plus, Twitter, Facebook, and LinkedIn. Our Vision is to create a movement advocating uplifting leadership and changing lives. Our mission is to help leaders become better leaders by providing a forum where members can connect, engage, serve, learn, and lead. These 5 words represent the Essentials of Lead With Giants. Our name is derived from this quote attributed to Sir Isaac Newton in 1676: 'If I have seen farther than others, it is because I was standing on the shoulder of giants.' Of the various platforms, Google Plus is the most engaged, followed by Twitter, Facebook, and LinkedIn. I'm proud to say that Lead With Giants has a reputation as a community offering robust engagement. Epictetus said, 'The key is to keep company only with people who uplift you, whose presence calls forth your best.' Global social media networks allow for the creation of meaningful communities that change lives and make a real difference in the world. Lead With Giants is an example of such a community.

I have connected with many wonderful people from around the world in this community and am making plans to connect in person with some members from Scotland and the USA who are coming to Australia soon.

Events

Google Events allows you to plan an event or hangout (figure 12.17).

Figure 12.17: Google Events

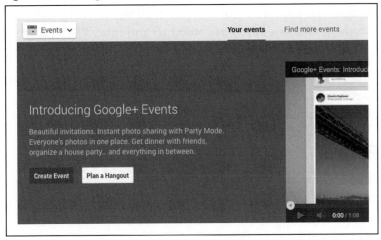

Hangouts

Hangouts are free group video calls (figure 12.18).

Figure 12.18: Google+ Hangouts

You can hang out on video with up to nine other people in a Google Hangout. The on-air version allows you to produce a live show that is directly recorded to YouTube. This is a great way to share information or teach customers about a product.

You can also tune in to live video broadcasts on topics that matter to you. A schedule of upcoming Hangouts On Air is provided through Google.

Pages

Some 97 per cent of consumers search for local businesses online, and a Google Plus Page will ensure they know where you are and can follow a map or click a phone number to reach you (figure 12.19).

Figure 12.19: Google+ Pages for companies

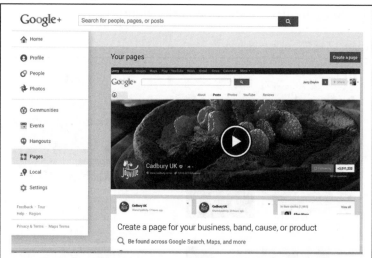

Customers can show their appreciation through ratings and reviews, use the +1 button to endorse your content, and re-share your posts across the web. Again this is more a function for marketers but if you're a small business it's easy to do. Go to Google Pages and follow the prompts.

Google Local

Remember that Google has already mapped the world and this information is freely available to anyone who wants to use it.

But we also know that people like to shop local. Google Plus allows you to list yourself in their local pages and business reviews. If you're a local business, localisation has many benefits (figure 12.20).

Figure 12.20: Google+ Local

This chapter will get you up and running on Google Plus, but once you've learned the ropes you may want to amp it up with some bootcamp suggestions. These are pro tips. I've included sources for these great tips so you can look up authorities and follow their other fabulous suggestions.

Google Plus bootcamp

- IFTTT.com enables you to take a trigger ('If this [happens]') and create an action ('...then that [happens]') by creating recipes: 'If I get a Gmail from so-and-so, post this page'. You can integrate this with Google+ by creating an RSS feed that can be used within IFTTT. (Martin Shervington)

- Track how widely any post is shared with Google+ Ripples by clicking the small arrow at the top right of a post; selecting it will show you a scalable chart showing how your post has spread. (JR Raphael)

- One amazing thing about Hangouts is interacting with people speaking different languages. Translate them using Google's 'Listen' feature. (Jared S, HostDime)

- Bookmark your favourite posts by using Circles. Create an empty circle called 'Favourite Posts' (or whatever you like) from the 'Find people' tab, then share everything you find interesting to this circle. You can bring up a post from the circle at any time by choosing it from the top of your stream and sharing its unique URL. (David Nield, Gizmodo)

- Tweak your email notification options to reduce Gmail traffic by going to Google Account options and unchecking all of the ones you don't want to get. (Patrick Miller, *PC World*)

- Search for interesting stuff to share about particular topics in the Sparks section on the side menu of the main page. Click Sparks, and search for things that you're interested in. Pin a search on your sidebar for easy future access by clicking the Add Interest button under the search field. (Patrick Miller, *PC World*)

- Add a poll to a published post by instructing your readers to +1 to vote, and then quickly add comments containing the choices. Afterwards, select 'Disable Comments' from your post menu to encourage voting. (Webdesignerdepot)

Chapter summary

Google Plus is like a social layer across life as you know it, adding connectivity to search, maps, YouTube, email, apps, games and music, to name but a few.

You can share information exclusively or widely, hang out with an individual or group at a moment's notice or drop into a videocast you like the sound of.

It's a great way to grow the prominence of your business locally but also to extend its reach globally. Google Plus organises the world's information, and you are a part of that world.

CHAPTER 13

Facebook: your new lounge

As in real life, so online. You used to have family and friends around to your house to catch up. You'd update each other and share holiday snaps. Now your family and friends are scattered around the world. You still share updates and photos but you do so on Facebook. Facebook is your new lounge.

A Facebook snapshot

It's	a social network
Started	2004
Current number of users	1.25 billion and counting
Important because	comments made here influence decisions
Worrying because	they've breached privacy

The backstory

The rise and rise of Facebook is like some sort of strange mash-up: startup fantasy meets college-humour flick, smart techy teenagers develop a popular but ultimately useless invention and get rich.

Sounds fun but much like a recipe for a fad, which is why many executives spent so long ignoring or dismissing it as the purview of kids. As the saying goes in social media (with a smiling emoticon to set the tone): #*fail*.

For anyone still anchored by the origins of this story, here's the update.

The social network was indeed started by Harvard college students in 2003, originally as 'Facemash', which allowed students to compare photographs of fellow students side by side and choose who was 'hot or not'. Founder Mark Zukerberg later applied the same idea to an art history project, uploading images and opening them to comments from classmates. What became clear was that whether it was of girls or Augustan art, the ability to view an image and immediately respond and share a view struck a chord with users.

Fast forward to 2014, Facebook is now a corporate giant with 1.25 billion users around the world. And at 10 years old—a long time in any business these days, let alone technology—it's certainly surpassed fad status (http://expandedramblings.com /index.php/by-the-numbers-17-amazing-facebook-stats/).

On their own, numbers are easy to dismiss. But if you stop to think about it, the network is almost as populous as the two largest countries in the world, China and India. I don't know where you live but here in Australia we're edging towards 23 million citizens, relatively insignificant when compared with Facebook numbers.

With size comes reach. Already Facebook hosts over 80 million business pages, and that's just from the more adventurous businesses or brands where marketers have been able to convince decision-makers of the value. Although there are more alternatives now than there were when the network erupted, as business becomes more comfortable with social engagement, the number of pages will surely grow.

Facebook also has the largest collection of online photos—around 240 billion on its server, with 350 million new photos uploaded each day. Although the love of video and photography is not slowing down, people's preferences around managing images seem to be. Snapchat, for example, deletes photographs as soon as they are viewed, which has proved extremely popular with young users.

As for the baby-faced college kid, CEO Mark Zuckerberg is now a 30-year old billionaire leading 6000 employees of a listed company worth $100 billion (although obviously views about its true value vary considerably). Now the company faces legal action on a number of fronts, from charges of violating federal wiretap laws to a nationwide class action tracking cookie lawsuit, and has been investigated by Ireland's Data Protection Commissioner (DPC) for privacy breaches. Zuckerberg's company is also caught in the broader net of privacy issues facing US technology companies alleged to have illegally shared the private details of users with the National Security Agency (NSA) as part of their secret surveillance program known as PRISM.

Not such a fairytale anymore. And as for any mature business, changing times deliver risk as well as opportunities.

Right now many young users are migrating away from Facebook to platforms like Snapchat and Twitter. Of course millions of new users are also signing on. Interestingly, one of the fastest growing demographics on Facebook is people aged 45–54, which jumped 46 per cent in 2013. It's probably no surprise that as adults become more adventurous about social networks their progeny will look elsewhere. But when they do it's to a better alternative social media network, not away from social media.

Facebook is constantly evolving its offering in response to the changing environment and user preferences. In 2013 the platform introduced Graph Search, which is equivalent to a search engine (like Google) within the platform. Graph allows you to search the data of friends in your account — say, for that restaurant you vaguely recall someone posting about when they were in Vietnam. Users can also search topics in real time. For example, you can search up a particular sports game and connect to conversations people in your network are having about it, much like sitting around the TV with mates, only with fast forward.

In response to what seems like an unstoppable global appetite for video and photo content, Facebook bought Instagram with its 150 million monthly users to integrate into its offering.

Issues plaguing the giant may not go away easily but neither, it seems, will Facebook.

The impacts on business

Remember all those people who held out against buying mobile phones? Their dogged determination to prevent people from being able to reach them unless they were home? The idea that someone phoning if they were in a shopping centre or at the beach would diminish their quality of life? In retrospect, we reflect on these concerns as silly, but at the time many shared their fears.

Things have moved on and we have all adapted, as humans tend to do. There are now more mobile phones than there are people on Earth, and most of us feel anxious if we leave the phone behind when we're on the move. Whether you think this is good or bad, it's just the way it is. So too with Facebook. You may like it or loathe it, use or refuse it, but for billions of people around the world, it's how they connect.

Which brings us to the impacts of Facebook for business. This is something that every executive needs to understand because the ubiquity of the network impacts the people in our business, our customers and the ways in which we do business (marketing, communication, customer services, research and sales).

This is not a book about Facebook for business (there are many), so my aim is simply to make you aware of some of the key issues that business leaders are facing in this space. They include:

1   Facebooking on the job

2   productivity impacts

3   core hours (the professional/personal divide)

4   the new recruiter.

Facebooking on the job

Facebook is likely being used throughout your organisation. People will be using it at work and after hours, on their personal devices and on devices that the business owns. It will be running in the background on many computers all day, sometimes passively. This is, or should be, the assumed and agreed starting point for any discussion. On what comes next, there's wild disagreement.

One problem is that people are trying to find ways to squeeze the management of social behaviour into existing business frameworks, rather than questioning whether existing business frameworks are still relevant to the way we live. This is a more difficult question because it requires us to rethink organisational policies at the deeper level. My view is that in the coming times, whether or not we want to, we will have to face this question.

Some organisations have taken a hard line towards social networks, preventing staff from accessing them during work hours. The reason? To ensure employees remain focused and productive.

But what is really going on? People are checking them anyway. Instead of doing so openly at their desk they're taking sneak peeks at their mobile phones. Socialising has always been one of the pleasures of work, whether it's a chat at the water cooler or sharing morning tea. It may look a bit different, but it's the same idea.

At the same time, businesses need to manage time and in certain industries distraction can be a health and safety hazard. Executives need to strike a balance. All too often, though, senior executives who are out of step with their people are making decisions. I know that's a bitter pill to swallow, but bear with me.

The reality is that if you believe Facebook is a waste of time, then you're unlikely to be amenable to a policy that allows people to access it from their desktop. And when someone challenges a core belief in which we've invested, at least in part, some of our identity, the tendency is to come out swinging.

We've all been there. When I took my previous organisation into social media in 2006 we were considered to be ahead of the curve. This was not because I fully understood the value. As far back as 1997 social style sites such as Six Degrees (now folded) were allowing users to set up their own and surf others' profiles. These were people who could really see what was coming. I was fortunate to meet a number of individuals who opened my eyes to the value of these platforms, especially at organisational levels. Once I moved past resistance and started to read deeply about trends, review data and experiment, my views could be found down the end of the corridor, to the left—those views were turned on their head.

Productivity impacts

Creating productive teams and profitable outcomes (if you're a for-profit) is the game, so concerns about productivity are understandable. But there is little evidence to suggest social media diminishes productivity. Despite this, it is often cited as a time waster.

What it does bring to light is that many productivity measures continue to emphasise inputs over outputs. A widget-focused leadership mindset will not equip managers to deal with the emerging complexity of the digital and social age.

There is research that suggests social media can enhance engagement, which is a key element of productivity. It's well recognised, for example, that young professionals value internet connection above even a pay rise. A recent Cisco study found companies that embraced social media during business hours were more attractive to job applicants in highly competitive talent pools. It's tempting to think of social networking as a concession to Millennials but the adoption of social media across all age groups suggests otherwise.

The value of digital to productivity means measuring direct contributions from pure online businesses but also the indirect activity of mixed businesses, including the use of social media for engagement, sales and customer service.

Core hours

We've all worked with them, the people who turn up at 7 am and throw disdainful glances at their colleagues as they arrive any time after, signalling disapproval with a glance at their watch or a dramatic sigh. Normally they're reading the newspaper or they're on the social round, but with the office light on and computer buzzing it's clear they at least are serious.

This is the culture of input over output and one deeply entrenched in the notion of core hours. But what are core hours in 2014?

The distinction between personal and professional life has changed dramatically since the advent of the eight-hour workday, introduced as a result of the industrial revolution. We answer emails from colleagues at midnight and check Facebook at 11 am. Or prepare a PowerPoint while watching TV and status update our mates straight after we walk out of the performance review. The 10 minutes we lose between 9 and 5 we make up for between dinner and going to bed. Whether you think this is good or bad for us as a society, it's what we do. The days of a sharp demarcation between our personal and work lives are gone, and I imagine the line will become even fuzzier as globalisation and interconnection increases.

This makes it very difficult to measure productivity by time within core hours. It also suggests that in future we need to concentrate our energies (where appropriate, of course—this cannot apply in every industry) on developing Key Result Areas that more accurately measure what people achieve.

The new recruiter

Here's something else Zuckerberg may not have been thinking about when he hacked into Harvard databases to steal photographs: that Facebook would become one of the most powerful and popular recruitment tools, on both the buy and sell side of the equation.

Intuitively it makes sense. People within our network, usually family and friends, refer the majority of jobs. And a lot of those are now on Facebook. Then of course there's LinkedIn, but I've already devoted a chapter to that.

I've seen Facebook work firsthand many times. While I was writing this chapter a friend who had been travelling for seven months (naturally we followed her around the world as she posted photos from wherever she was) got home and reached out for work. She simply wrote in her status update that she was on the lookout and within seconds the first comment came back. When I checked at the end of the day there were welcome backs and jokes about a less indulgent time ahead, warm leads—and by the end of the narrative she'd pretty much been offered part-time work (granted, not in her field) to get her going while she looked around. Not bad for 100 words posted from a café.

I've used my networks for colleagues in similar ways, in particular those who have not yet built their own. Recently the head of a PR agency specialising in what we would call traditional communications had to act fast when a client requested an online community manager as part of an engagement project. I posted with the key words #jobs #Melbourne #ORM and within a minute (yes, I am not exaggerating for dramatic effect) two viable candidates came back, one of whom ended up working on the project. Enough said.

But recruiters are also using social networks as part of locating, engaging with and checking potential recruits.

By the way, I don't think we'll see the recruitment industry disappearing as a result, although they are already changing the way they operate. While the advantages of interconnectivity include immediacy, openness and choice, the reality is we are very busy and are increasingly seeking 'curators' (including specialists) to manage the overwhelming choice on our behalf. But it does mean that, whether you're looking or being looked at, the importance of a visible and well-regarded profile in these platforms will become increasingly important.

Me 3.0

Should you be using Facebook for your personal platform? How visible you want to be on Facebook depends, as ever, on what you want to achieve.

If, for example, building a fan base is core to your personal brand strategy then it could be a good idea.

Australian fitness guru Michelle Bridges is an excellent example of a micromaven whose personal brand is also her business and who uses Facebook to share her real-life expertise with clients even when she is not 'there' physically (www.facebook .com/12WBT?fref=ts).

But I'm going to assume that like most executives you're 'working for the wo/man' and that while your marketers, communicators, and customer services and sales people should be studying every nuance, your use will be more limited.

I recommend that as an executive you think of it as your lounge. A place you are free to retreat to at the end of the day, and where it means something to the people who get to see and comment on photographs of the school concert. I love it for this. With almost no effort I can keep up with where people are and what they are doing. And I prefer this light but regular content to an older equivalent, the annual Christmas letter.

Personally, I apply the strictest privacy settings available on Facebook to all options and keep my sharing among friends. I've nonetheless set up Facebook pages for my business and personal blog as part of my 'secure your social media assets' strategy. I don't engage heavily on my business pages but time is a significant factor, and I imagine it is for you too.

So let's set up. Because this is for personal use I'm going to show you how to activate settings that will keep it just between those you choose. If you do want to friend a direct report, however, there are ways to limit the information they see.

Let's go — Facebook

Facebook is not an essential part of your personal professional platform, though if you're using it for business it's a must. That doesn't mean Facebook isn't popular (it's huge) or engaging (it's one of the most engaging networks on the planet). It's just that for busy executives, it's a place to go where you can close the door and leave work behind you, so to speak.

For that reason we're not going to spend too much time here, although I will give you a quick snapshot of how to set up Facebook and some things to look out for.

First head to Facebook.com. Sign up using your email (figure 13.1). Remember this is a Facebook account, so that's you personally (though a business can also create a Facebook Page). Facebook requires you to use your real name.

Fill out the level of detail you're comfortable with. I leave a lot out here because my friends already know who I am. However, adding detail allows Facebook to make associations and suggestions that you might value. For example, if you fill in the name of the school you went to, Facebook will go through its databases to bring you suggestions of others who went there during that time. It could be a great way to reconnect with a past friend.

Figure 13.1: Facebook's Home page

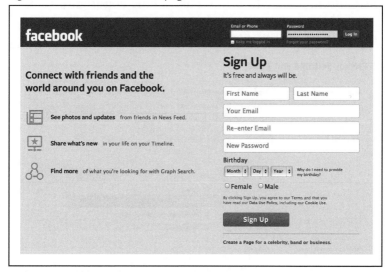

One thing you need to be conscious of in Facebook is choosing the right privacy settings. Because we're not using it for marketing, we're going to shut it down to friends only. To adjust these settings click on the padlock icon to open up to Privacy Shortcuts (figure 13.2).

Figure 13.2: Facebook privacy settings

You can adjust settings for every part of Facebook, and you'll have to do each manually. Just open up the Edit button. Choose Friends. You can customise what you want to share by opening the Custom icon, which looks like a little cog (figure 13.3).

Figure 13.3: locking down privacy to Friends

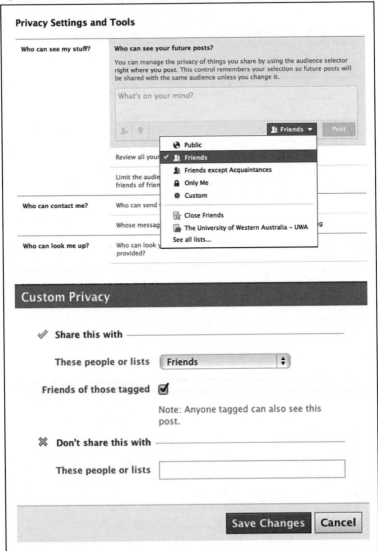

You can also edit all your security settings (figure 13.4).

Figure 13.4: security settings

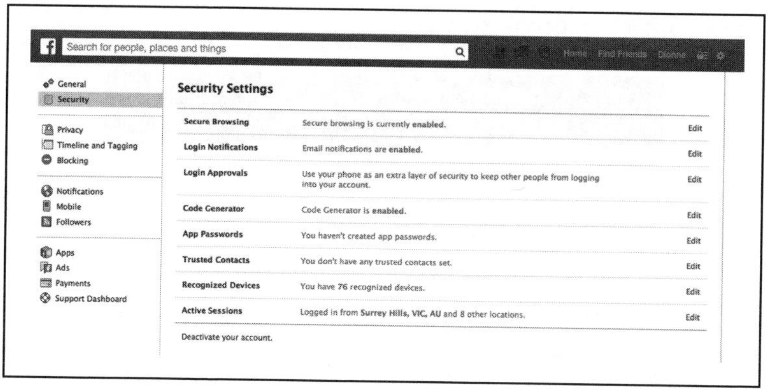

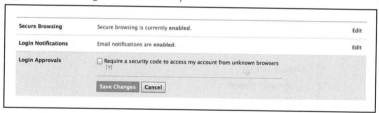

If you want to apply additional layers of security, such as a security code if your account is accessed from unknown browsers, just tick the box (figure 13.5).

Figure 13.5: adding levels of security

Facebook is easy to navigate. You can search within the Facebook network by using the Search icon (figure 13.6).

Figure 13.6: search function

The People icon allows you find and accept friends.

The Chat icon is your inbox. This is private and you can communicate with anyone you're connected to.

Find Friends allows you to search for people based on a number of criteria (figure 13.7).

Figure 13.7: search people criteria

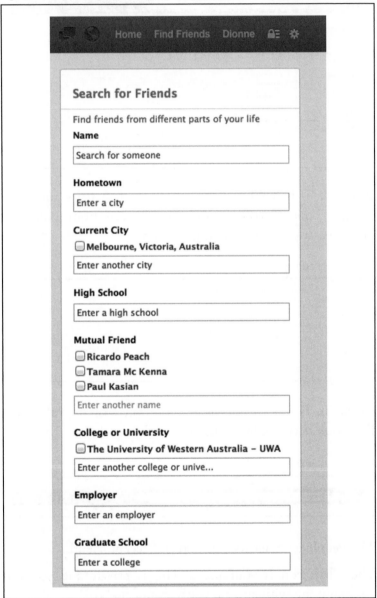

And your Home page can be found under your name (figure 13.8).

Figure 13.8: your Home page

You'll see that I am using a non-professional photo here; that's because it's for friends rather than colleagues.

Here you can see your timeline, photos, friends and a number of other options.

This chapter will get you up and running on Facebook, but once you've learned the ropes you may want to amp it up with some bootcamp suggestions. These are pro tips. I've included sources for these great tips so you can look up authorities and follow their other fabulous suggestions.

Facebook bootcamp

- Although we're using Facebook as a lounge, if you're an entrepreneur or self-employed executive you may want to build influence here, because Facebook is great for marketing.

- Your cover image size should be 851 pixels by 315 pixels and may not include more than 20 per cent text. (Genevieve Lachance, *Social Media Today*)

- Share videos, not just still images. (Emeric Ernoult, *Social Media Examiner*)

- Create and manage an event on Facebook. This will help you reach your contacts and track their interest. (Josh Cantone, Mashable)

- Click on the icon in the upper right of each post and choose 'Pin to top' from the drop-down menu. From then on your post of choice will always be at the top of your page, no matter what you post afterwards. (Glyn Dewis)

- Post a picture and ask followers to post versions of their own or anything that will encourage them to post images as replies. (Andrew Gough)

Chapter summary

Facebook is a social networking phenomenon with more than 1.25 billion users. Executives must understand the issues associated with this platform, including its impact on communication inside and outside work.

Facebook is vital for business marketing, although for busy executives who want to balance the private and public it has a different function.

You used to catch up and share photos with family and friends; you still do, but because many are now scattered around the world you do so on Facebook. It's your new social media lounge.

CHAPTER 14

Executive Ecosystem: curate, automate, bring it together

Now everything is up and running it's time to create an Executive Ecosystem. As you bring the different networks together they will leverage off one another, really cranking up your influence.

It's also time to take a breath.

We'll use the Buffer automation you started when you set up Twitter, which will allow you to post across international time zones and extend your reach while not being there personally. The beauty of this system is you can dive into your networks randomly or on a schedule, depending on your personality.

Executives have notoriously packed schedules. Buffer helps you fit social into a busy life, although I would add that I think you should check social first, before email or other channels. When I get swamped with work and writing deadlines and am short of time, I temporarily withdraw from some of the excellent and engaged communities I belong to in Google Plus that require thoughtful (read more time-intense) responses. I also don't open my inbox, but I do check my Twitter feed. People I know understand this so they reach me there.

Creating an Executive Ecosystem is like getting all the divisions of your organisation at the same table. As with any great team this generates synergy.

Some social media influences (who I respect) are against any form of automation, believing that when you post you should be there to respond immediately. I understand this point of view but it's not always practical; I've found that realistically people don't mind waiting to hear back. Everyone understands that it's sleep time somewhere in the world. This is a personal platform, not a customer service channel. Scheduling combined with personal engagement is not automation. As to a completely automated, outsourced platform—why bother? By all means get a consultant or PR firm to help you with administrative management, setup and training, but engaging is about the real you.

There are many wonderful curating and automating tools. I'll list some that come highly recommended at the end of the chapter. But as I said at the start of this book, I want to provide you with a practical system, not a list of options that will leave you feeling overwhelmed. For that reason, I am sharing the system I use. There are others, but I know this works well, allowing the right balance of bot and brain.

Scoop.it

It's chaos out there. In a single *minute* on the web:

- 11 000 professional searches are done on LinkedIn
- 347 new blogs are posted
- 571 websites are created
- 278 000 tweets are sent
- 2 million searches are made on Google

- 216 000 photos are shared on Instagram
- $83 000 of sales take place on Amazon
- three days' worth of video is uploaded to YouTube.

And I'm homing in on what happens in 60 seconds in just a few areas because I didn't want to throw a statistics grenade.

It's also going to get louder and more unruly as time goes on. To be heard, visible and respected you must curate excellent content, the kind of content you would have gone to the trouble of photocopying to give to a friend or colleague 10 years ago, because you knew they'd love it.

That's curation and as we go deeper and deeper into the information age, great curators will thrive. We all love to know the go-to source, the material that matters, the analysis based on current, cutting-edge research and not pulp fiction. These people know how to source, select and share the gold. And I am going to teach you to do the same.

Scoop.it is a great curation platform and the one I use.

You tell it what you want it to search for by entering keywords, from broad brush (technology trends, drones, manufacturing) to narrow (3D printing, nanotechnology, atomic specific manufacturing). You can also add in specific sources, and again they can be very wide (Google) or very narrow (the list of a specific Twitter influencer whose work you appreciate). Curating curators in this way is a powerful way to ensure that what you post sets you apart.

Scoop.it serves up everything it has found in a nice list under a bold heading and a snapshot of the content. You then click — yes or no, add a comment or not — and push it out onto whatever social network you like. The great thing is that Scoop.it supports Buffer, so you can push all that content into your Buffer and it will come out bit by bit across the week on whatever channel you choose.

I spend a significant part of my Sunday reading, thinking about what I am reading, commenting and then adding it into whatever social media channel I think is appropriate. I know that irrespective of what happens during the week, I am sharing great material with my constituents. The rest I do on the run, checking Twitter over coffee in the morning or from my phone between meetings, whenever it works. This approach will work well for you too.

Setting up Scoop.it

Go to Scoop.it. Join. You will be asked to use social sign-in. I use Twitter. Scoop.it needs your permission to connect via Twitter so agree. The first time you use Scoop.it you'll be asked to set up an account. Do so (figure 14.1).

On Scoop.it you curate content according to topics. You can choose five topics. Really think about what content you want to share. The tighter your focus the tighter the content that will be sourced and the more interest you'll get from a community interested in the subject. The aim is not for volume here but relevance.

Figure 14.1: setting up Scoop.it

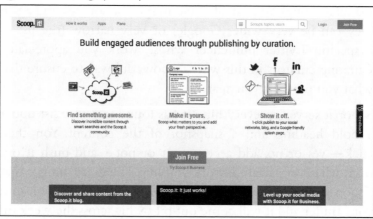

(continued)

Figure 14.1: *(cont'd)*

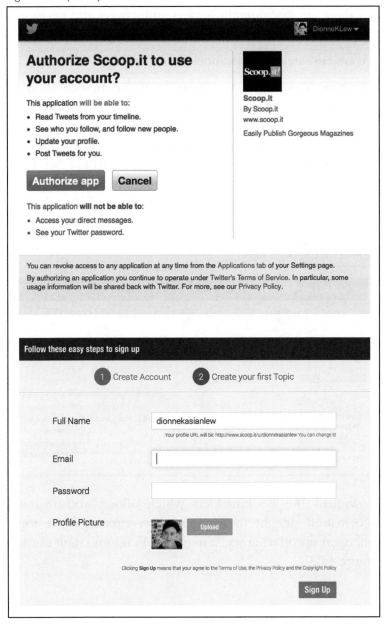

For example, if only 10 people view a curation on Patent Trolls, but these are key thought leaders, influencers and decisions-makers in this area, your job is done.

We are saturated in generalities. Stand out.

Your topic should be clear (figure 14.2). No mystical allusions please, no one is going to open a curation they don't understand. There's no time. I have used really targeted keywords — patent assertion entity (PAE), non-practising entities (NPEs), patent law, Unified Patent Court, unitary patent, SHIELD Act, High Court, Patents County Court, patent trolls and finally, more generally, social media law. This is because I want to draw in related issues that may be slightly off tangent but interesting.

Figure 14.2: creating a topic

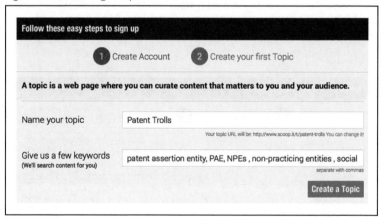

Download the bookmarklet, which allows you to send information straight to Scoop.it. Start curating. Your topic will open up, offering you a number of customisation options (figure 14.3).

Figure 14.3: installing the bookmarklet

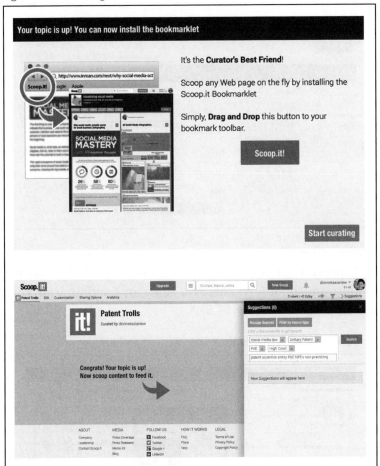

Edit or modify the global parameters of your topic — here you can add detail (figure 14.4, overleaf). You'll also add the URL for your patent troll topic. Remember to save any changes you make. You can also delete a topic here.

Figure 14.4: set the parameters of your topic

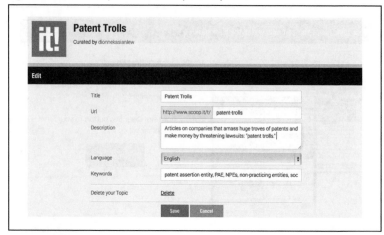

Cutomisation allows you to create your own style, which is important for a personal professional brand. Use similar colours and photos so there's a sense of continuity in your digital footprint (figure 14.5).

Figure 14.5: branding Scoop.it

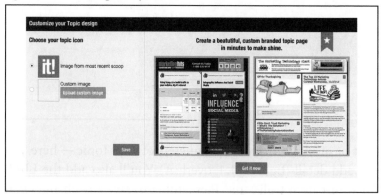

Sharing means in your social media networks (figure 14.6). This is critical because it means you can go to Scoop. it every morning and cover everything you need to, other than checking in on the @Notifications section of Twitter (remember this is your inbox) when you have time.

Figure 14.6: link with social share buttons

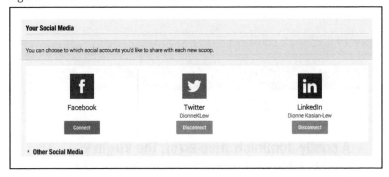

Analytics, as it suggests, gives you data.

Scoop.it will now start to curate content for you. On the right-hand side you will see all the content it pulls in (figure 14.7).

Figure 14.7: Scoop.it suggestions appear

Open up the content. If you like it, Scoop.it. This means it is going into your topic where it will be stored in your collection, a bit like putting aside interesting newspaper articles in a file.

You can offer a personal perspective, and this adds value. What you write here will be posted in your Facebook and LinkedIn status updates if you decide to share them there. Twitter will update as shown. You can edit in any way you like.

Tick the networks you want to share it to and push the Publish button (figure 14.8).

Figure 14.8: adding a comment

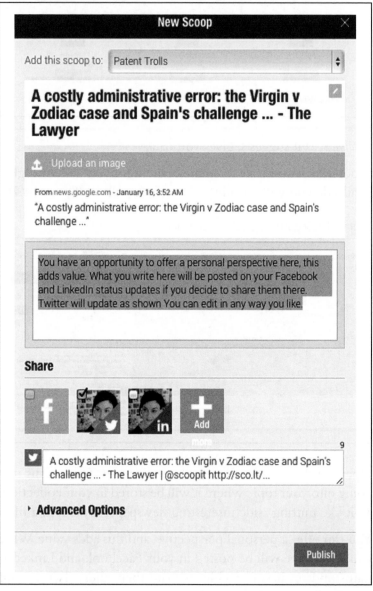

(continued)

Figure 14.8: *(cont'd)*

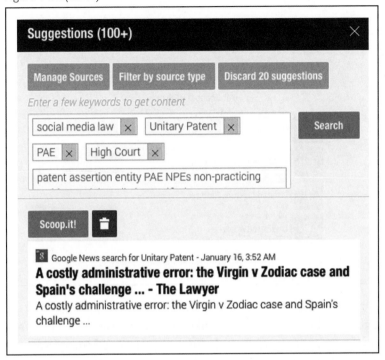

Scoop.it will offer you a premium option (figure 14.9, overleaf). Unless you're against it and want to use the free option, sign up. I use premium because I like to use my Buffer. The additional social account access allows me to post from Scoop.it to Buffer.

I can curate to my heart's content when I have time but allow the content to come out bit by bit during the week. This is what you want. To build influence you need a constant presence but you absolutely don't want to:

- serve up junk

- spam people with scores of articles and then go suddenly quiet.

Think of the real-life equivalents — tedious gossip, interrupting, silence. Not a great formula for building engagement.

Figure 14.9: offer for Scoop.it PRO

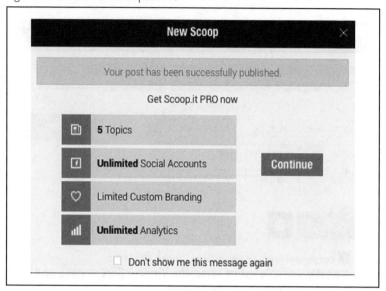

Manage sources is available only with the paid version of Scoop.it, but it can really make your life easy. You can search sources or create advanced source options. Advanced sources are really the heart of your influence strategy (figure 14.10).

Figure 14.10: managing sources

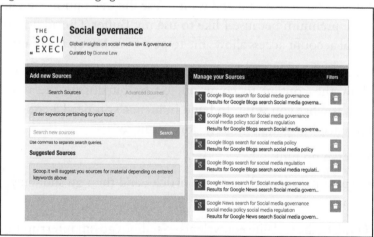

(continued)

Figure 14.10: *(cont'd)*

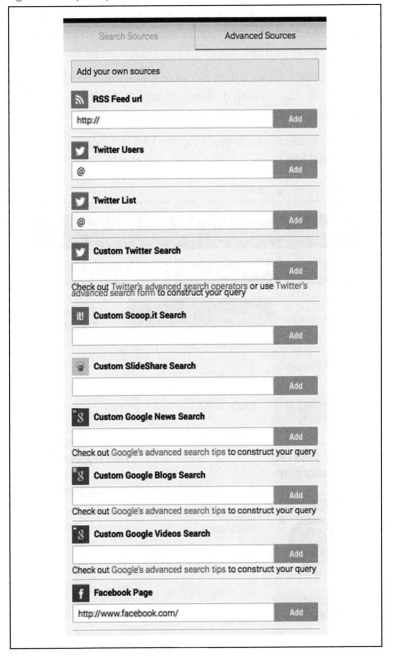

Add the social media networks of influencers, pull in their content and share it. Add Twitter lists—your own or others'. Again, you can focus the content tightly on people you want to get to know without having to think about and go back to your Twitter lists.

You can even add in other Scoop.it curations, working with members of the Scoop.it community to create a powerful information source.

And you can filter your sources (figure 14.11). Clicking on which source you'd like to see content from will eliminate other sources.

Figure 14.11: filtering sources

Trash any content that's not relevant, and scoop and publish content that is, sharing it immediately or pushing it into Buffer (figure 14.12).

Figure 14.12: scoop relevant content

Keep scooping. You'll see all your great material curated under your topic (figure 14.13). People can now come to this topic and read and add their own insights.

Figure 14.13: curated content keeps accumulating

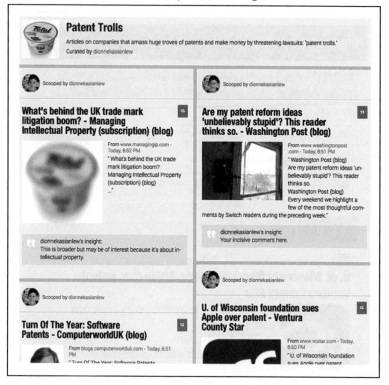

On the top right you'll find your settings. Fill them out as usual (figure 14.14).

Figure 14.14: complete your settings

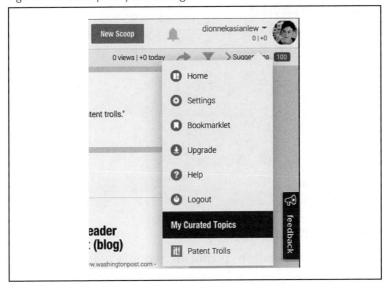

If you need additional help just head to the Help section and watch the videos (figure 14.15).

That's it.

Figure 14.15: the help section

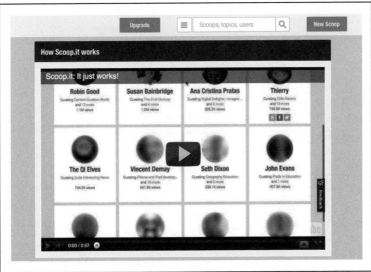

Beyond Scoop.it

Other curation or bookmarking sites include:

- Paper.li
- Bundlr
- Storify
- Sulia
- Learnist
- Storyful
- Evernote.

Chapter summary

Integrate the curation platform Scoop.it with scheduling tools to create a powerful professional platform. A professional platform synthesises sources and social networks, creates strategic and random connections, and grows your visibility and influence in a way that works for busy executives, ensuring maximum impact for minimum time.

Conclusion

The Social Executive promise fulfilled

Executives who have been asking why social media is important for business and how to involve themselves now have some answers.

The Social Executive presents powerful evidence from the best consultancies around the world on the value of the connected economy and its predicted growth.

In these chapters you've learned:

- to separate the fact from fiction on social media
- that it's not a fad, a young person's game or merely for posting photos of lunch, but a powerful professional and business tool to be applied across every industry and area of the business
- that social media is a deeply entrenched form of communication that is still growing rapidly and turning the way we do business on its head
- that there's strong evidence in support of investing in social business in your industry
- to challenge past perceptions and adopt a social media mindset
- what the key social media platforms are and how to use them

- how to use social media for professional development
- about some key legal and corporate governance issues that executives need to manage through sound policies and practices
- to establish and grow a Professional Platform.

A Professional Platform will help you establish and grow online influence and leverage your existing expertise and experience in new ways.

As I said at the start, there's no mystique to social media. But there is magic. As in real life, so in the digital realm. I look forward to meeting you there.

Now let's schedule your ongoing social strategy in a practical way.

Your social strategy
Daily
Twitter

1   Go to @Notifications in Twitter if you can, see who's connected with you, reply and engage in conversation.

LinkedIn

2   Check your LinkedIn inbox.

3   LinkedIn will notify you if someone comments on a status update — respond if you can.

4   If you have time to look at content in a LinkedIn group that's well set up and active, do.

Google Plus

5   Notifications from your network will appear in the Social section. You'll be signalled if you're mentioned. You will also receive notifications from communities. Respond if you can.

Weekly
Twitter

6   Clean up your Twitter stream using ManageFlitter or a similar hygiene tool.

7   Follow people you like on Twitter who have followed you.

8   Do a 'big follow' if you can by going to the following of someone whose feed you admire and connecting with their followers.

LinkedIn

9   Respond to invitations.

10   Reach out to networks.

11   Choose one group that you believe will really add professional value. Read material and make comments.

Google Plus

12   Scan the ecosystem and +1 posts you like.

13   If you're in a community, spend time reading content and commenting on it or posting content that you find interesting and that's relevant to that community.

Scoop.it

14   Read, comment and scoop content. Share immediately through relevant social media networks or push content into your buffer.

Monthly
SlideShare

15   Do you have a presentation to share on SlideShare? Remember to save it as a PDF, and ensure it makes sense without a presenter to explain it.

#SOMETHINGMORE

Social media etiquette

Yes, rules are made to be broken, and I'd rather you take a playful and experimental approach to your social media platforms than become a cookie-cut automaton who is boring and not worth time and attention. Having said that, there are some basic principles in relation to how to engage online that I think are worth adopting.

These should be familiar to you. I could say, 'As in real life, so online', and assume you always behave well, but we know that different contexts support different types of behaviour. For example, even though you're both a pedestrian and a motorist, you behave differently when you're on foot and when you're behind the wheel. When you're on foot you probably glare at the driver who is trying to push into the intersection as you cross at your own pace, and when you're the driver you sit there impatiently, wishing the pedestrian who seems to be deliberately sauntering would just hurry up.

So here are some of the benchmarks of good social media behaviour:

- *Be polite.* Remember to say please and thank you. We don't like being taken for granted in real life, and online it's the same. There's a human being on the other side of every comment.

- *Give more than you take.* When you find material you know someone else will love, send it to them. Ask them about themselves. When they ask a question, respond. Of course there are exceptions, and I'm not suggesting you should listen endlessly to someone who is determined to drone on and drain your energy, but there's way too much me, me, me out there. Give a little. No, give a lot. If your mindset is always to share something of value with others, then you are creating a lot of great social karma (using that word loosely).

- *Listen more than you speak.* Be interested in people, and listen to what they are saying. You will learn more from listening to what customers, connections and friends are saying than from trying to promote yourself. That's so boring.

- *Think reciprocity.* The best relationships in life happen when the intention of each towards the other is good. Although 'win–win' was overused in the eighties, it's just as powerful an approach to business now as then and, let's face it, throughout history. Mutual benefit. As my wonderful friend Kare Anderson says (follow her @kareanderson), 'Mutuality matters'.

- *Be who you are.* But do so consciously. As a tool, social media amplifies your presence and message. If you're fun-loving and frivolous then there's no point presenting yourself as serious. If you're serious and analytical, cut the 'awesome'. Be authentic but also aware of how you impact others. Self-awareness is critical at work and in life—and online, where people don't have the benefit of body language and tone when communicating.

Now a few behaviours to avoid:

- *Shun controversy*. It's so tempting to dive in when there's
  a trending issue that you're passionate about, but unless
  it's core to your values and how you present yourself
  publicly (for me that would be *equality*), be careful. Issues
  that cause controversy are typically complex and require
  analysis, patience and the right conditions to be genuinely
  discussed. One-liners can really backfire. You also learn
  quickly that some issues you don't consider controversial
  can seem highly provocative to others. Many a person has
  been sacked because their racist or sexist comments did
  not reflect the values of the company they worked for, and
  many of those people thought they were joking.

- *Don't be sarcastic*. I'm loath to say don't joke because some
  good, clean mucking around can be fun. I am saying,
  though, that you need to tread carefully. Social media
  platforms are a bit like texts, in that you cannot read the
  tone and have no visual clues. Remember, the person on
  the other side of the world does not know if you're up or
  down, if you had a good or bad day. I once had trouble
  sending a response in my Twitter direct mail to someone
  who had asked me a question, so I sent him a tweet saying
  I was having a problem with DM. He took it that I meant
  my 'problem' was that he was speaking to me there, and
  being a very respectful person he immediately withdrew.
  I had to explain that the glitch was technical—that
  Twitter was no longer allowing me to send links. Even the
  most innocent communication can be misconstrued. So
  be mindful.

- *Don't be negative*. Ever been out to lunch with someone
  who complained about the weather, public transport, their
  boss, their team, their kids, the trip over to see you, the

service, the food? It's a sure route to feeling depleted and drained. These are not people you should spend much time with. Best to allow them to find others of like mind rather than allowing them to feed off your energy. Don't go in, don't go in and don't go in. (Of course, saccharine people can be just as draining. Stick with authentic people.)

- *Cut the spin.* It's great that so many people are getting online, but the downside is that many corporates think it's a new place to put your spin. Don't do it. While you're here as a person you are also a representative of your company. If a customer complains that their parcel has not arrived, don't say, 'We regret your experience and advise that on average we successfully deliver 1 billion parcels each year'. They don't care, and nor should they. Here's an alternative suggestion: 'Really sorry to hear that, can you tell me a bit more using DM?' The customer is not always right and I am not for a second suggesting you defer to everyone, but let's cut the scripts. Please.

Checklists

Owning digital assets

☐ Have you bought your domain name and variations from a domain name registrant? There are plenty around, such as Hover, GoDaddy, CrazyDomains, Namecheap, Dreamhost, Name, and 1&1 Internet.

☐ Try to use the same name wherever you can to create brand continuity.

☐ Choose a name that will give you longevity—not one that reflects only your current circumstances—for example, @dionnelew and not @dionnecoachSocialExec.

☐ Are you aware that different countries have different rules about what domains you can own? Check with the regulator in your country.

☐ Have you secured your Twitter handle?

☐ Have you secured your name on LinkedIn and customised your URL? Remember, first come first served here.

☐ Have you secured your name on Facebook? You can set up Pages associated with this account too.

☐ Have you secured a SlideShare account?

☐ Have you secured your name as a Gmail address and set up a Google Plus profile?

☐ Have you set up a Scoop.it account and claimed five interesting topics you want to be known for?

Online reputation management

☐ Have you bought your domain name?

☐ Have you set up an About.Me page? I won't go into details about how to do it because it's pretty intuitive and not an essential part of your platform, but a lot of people are using it as a de facto landing page. You can also create a Gravatar—or globally recognised avatar—by following the prompts at Gravatar.com.

☐ Are you on Twitter and using hashtags that clearly identify topics you want to be associated with?

☐ Do you have a well-written LinkedIn profile with credible recommendations?

☐ Have you set up a Google Alert with your name and that of your business?

☐ Have you set up two-step verification on your social media accounts where it's available?

☐ Do you have a password on your smartphone?

☐ Have you locked down your Facbeook privacy settings?

☐ Do you have the rights to the images you are using in SlideShare presentations?

Increase your Klout score

☐ Is your Twitter account public?

☐ Are all your social media platforms connected in settings?

☐ Do you engage with people on Twitter? Don't just post links.

☐ Do you have share buttons on your website, if you have one?

☐ Have you reached out to people in your niche who have a higher Klout score than you?

Index

So, what's next?

As I said at the start of this book, 'By the time you finish reading this book, the data will have changed...' And so it has!

Subscribe to dionnekasianlew.com and you'll receive regular updates on this fast-changing environment.

For more help and support consider...

Speaking
Book Dionne to talk with your Board or leadership, marketing and communications teams.

Consulting
Work with Dionne one-on-one.

Connect
You can reach Dionne at dionnekasianlew.com, email dionne@dionnekasianlew.com, through Twitter @dionnelew or LinkedIn http://www.linkedin.com /in/dionnelew and ask for help. She will be able to point you to influencers, research and tools or reach out through her networks to get you the help you need.

Learn more with practical advice from our experts

Digilogue
Anders Sörman-Nilsson

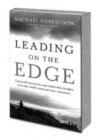

Leading on the Edge
Rachael Robertson

The Game Changer
Dr Jason Fox

Above the Line
Michael Henderson

microDOMINATION
Trevor Young

Lead with Wisdom
Mark Strom

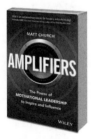

Amplifiers
Matt Church

Professional Services Marketing Wisdom
Ric Willmot

Web Marketing that Works
Adam Franklin and Toby Jenkins

Available in print and e-book formats

WILEY